WILKINSON'S

ROAD TRAFFIC OFFENCES

Second Cumulative Supplement to the Twenty-seventh Edition

General Editor
KEVIN McCORMAC, O.B.E., M.A.
of Gray's Inn, Barrister
Judge of the First-tier Tribunal

PHILIP BROWN, M.A., LL.B.
Former Senior Traffic Commissioner

PETER VEITS
District Judge (Magistrates' Courts)

NICK WATSON, O.B.E., LL.M., M.B.A.
District Judge (Magistrates' Courts)

JOANNA WOODHOUSE, M.A.
Judge of the First-Tier Tribunal

SWEET & MAXWELL

THOMSON REUTERS

Published in 2016 by Thomson Reuters (Professional) UK Limited trading as
Sweet & Maxwell, Friars House, 160 Blackfriars Road, London SE1 8EZ
(Registered in England & Wales. Company No. 1679046
Registered Office and address for service:
2nd floor, 1 Mark Square, Leonard Street, London EC2A 4EG)
For further information on our products and services, visit:
www.sweetandmaxwell.co.uk

Tables typeset by Servis Filmsetting Ltd, Manchester

All other typesetting by Sweet & Maxwell electronic system
Printed and bound in the UK by CPI Group (UK) Ltd, Croydon, CR04YY

No natural forests were destroyed to make this product;
only farmed timber was used and replanted.

A CIP catalogue record for this book is available from the British Library.

ISBN-9780414057234

Second Cumulative Supplement to the Twenty-seventh Edition 2016

Contents

Contents

Legislation

Preface

The law is generally stated as at August 1, 2016 — although, as is our custom, we have worked to later dates in some instances.

Since the First Supplement was published, consideration has been given to the application of the new statutory provisions regarding the extension to driving disqualifications. This is designed to ensure that those sentenced to custody experience the full period of disqualification following release. The Court of Appeal has helpfully addressed a number of the practical issues and we have provided coverage of that and also a flow chart which we believe will assist the busy practitioner.

More unusually, we have provided coverage of an extensive judgment of the Senior District Judge and Chief Magistrate Howard Riddle in which he has set out practical guidance needed to ensure the proper conduct of drink driving cases in magistrates' courts. This is a useful development in seeking to continue the emphasis on efficient management of all court proceedings.

There has also been a continuation of the steady stream of sentencing cases for the newly created offence of causing serious injury by dangerous driving recognising the difficulties caused by the relatively narrow range of sentence length arising from the lower maximum.

New publications referred to include the latest updates to the Criminal Procedure Rules and to the Magistrates' Court Sentencing Guidelines.

I continue to be grateful to the editorial team who contribute with erudition and thoroughness as we seek to produce a work of the highest quality. Thanks are also due to the staff at Sweet & Maxwell who provide professional support with regard to every aspect of production and publication.

Kevin McCormac
Worthing
September 2016

Table of Cases

Table of Cases

Table of Statutes

Table of Statutes

Table of Statutory Instruments

All entries are tabled to paragraph number.

Table of Statutory Instruments

Table of Statutory Instruments

Table of Statutory Instruments

Table of European Legislation

All entries are tabled to paragraph number.

Noter-up to Volume 1

Chapter 2—Procedure

Commencing Proceedings

Generally. In accordance with what has now become normal practice, the Crim-   **2.01**
inal Procedure Rules 2015 (SI 2015/1490) (as amended) have replaced the Criminal Procedure Rules 2014 (SI 2014/1610). The 2015 Rules came into effect on
October 5, 2015 and were amended by SI 2016/120 with effect from April 4,
2016: Criminal Procedure (Amendment) Rules 2016 and by SI 2016/705 with effect from October 3, 2016: Criminal Procedure (Amendment No.2) Rules 2016.
The rules were accompanied by new Criminal Practice Directions 2015 [2015]
EWCA 1567 (as amended: [2016] EWCA Crim 97). Few of the changes that
have been made affect the rules or the directions referred to in the main work
except for those noted within this Chapter. Unless specifically mentioned in this
supplement, the number and content of the rules described in the main work
remain the same. A main change in the Amendment No.2 Rules is the removal of
the word "written" in a number of places related to the provision of notices; this
reflects the move towards greater use of electronic transmission of information.

The relevant provision in the Criminal Procedure Rules 2015 (SI 2015/1490,
as amended) is r.46.1(2).

In accordance with s.29 of the Criminal Justice Act 2003, designated prosecu-   **2.02**
tors may institute criminal proceedings by issuing a written charge together with
a requisition (a requirement to attend before a specified magistrates' court) or a
single justice procedure notice. The designated prosecutors able to institute criminal proceedings and issue a single justice procedure notice (but not a requisition)
have been increased with effect from April 14, 2016 by the Criminal Justice Act
2003 (New Method of Instituting Proceedings) (Specification of Relevant
Prosecutors) Order 2016 (SI 2016/430). Now included are the Environment
Agency, most local authorities, the Natural Resources Body for Wales, and operators of tramcars on the Croydon Tramlink, the Manchester Metrolink and the
Nottingham Express Transit. Also included for a limited range of offences are
operators of "a railway asset" (railway offences) and the TV licensing authority
(offences relating to installation or use without a licence or obstruction of enforcement officers).

Jurisdiction over Offences

Initial Details of the Prosecution. The relevant provision in the Criminal Proce-   **2.51**
dure Rules 2015 (SI 2015/1490, as amended) is r.8.2.

3

Advice, Assistance and Representation

2.65 *Contempt of Court.* The relevant provision in the Criminal Procedure Rules 2015 (SI 2015/1490, as amended) is r.48.5.

The Hearing

2.111 *Notification of adjournment.* The relevant provisions in the Criminal Procedure Rules 2015 (SI 2015/1490, as amended) have changed and the reference to r.37 should be omitted.

2.121 *Initial Details of the Prosecution.* The relevant provision in the Criminal Procedure Rules 2015 (SI 2015/1490, as amended) is r.8.2.

2.134 *Summary trial.* The relevant provisions in the Criminal Procedure Rules 2015 (SI 2015/1490, as amended) are rr.24.3 and 24.4.

2.137 The relevant provision in the Criminal Procedure Rules 2015 (SI 2015/1490, as amended) is r.24.3.

2.140 The relevant provision in the Criminal Procedure Rules 2015 (SI 2015/1490, as amended) is r.24.3.

2.150 *Pleading guilty in writing.* The relevant provision in the Criminal Procedure Rules 2015 (SI 2015/1490, as amended) is Pt 16.

2.156 *Hearing charges together.* The relevant provision in the Criminal Procedure Rules 2015 (SI 2015/1490, as amended) is r.10(2).

2.158 The relevant provision in the Criminal Procedure Rules 2015 (SI 2015/1490, as amended) is r.10(2).

2.185 *Discontinuance of proceedings.* The relevant provision in the Criminal Procedure Rules 2015 (SI 2015/1490, as amended) is Pt 12.

Notices of Intended Prosecution

2.219 *Errors in the nature of the offence.* In the main work, we noted that prosecution for a less serious offence would not be expected to be a difficulty where the NIP specified a more serious offence. We are grateful to a correspondent for raising a question as to the position where the charge prosecuted is for a more serious offence than that noted in the NIP. Having been issued with an NIP for driving without due care and attention, a person had been charged with dangerous driving and the question was raised about the validity of the NIP. Reference was made to a Scottish case: *Procurator Fiscal, Aberdeen v Dalgarno* [2011] HCJAC 44, allowing a defence appeal in such circumstances.

Procedure

However, there do appear to be some surprising aspects to the judgment of the Scottish Appeal Court. The judgment (especially at [5]) refers to previous authority and identifies the primary purpose of the requirement to give warning as to "provide a prospective accused with notice within a reasonable time of an intention to prosecute", both to curtail any period of suspense and also to enable the accused to gather evidence when it is still fresh in the minds of any witnesses. However, the decision in the case itself appears to be based on the different sentencing provisions (one offence carrying mandatory disqualification but not the other), and on the fact that the defendant's legal representative appears to have overlooked the details of the instructions given by the client in relation to the offence he was prepared to plead guilty to.

Whilst there will clearly be circumstances where the offence charged and the offence specified in the NIP have markedly different characteristics, and a defendant may be prejudiced by not being told the actual offence, such prejudice may be less likely between dangerous and careless driving—both require driving below the standard provided by law, and the difference is simply the degree to which the driving falls below that standard. If ever tested, it therefore may be that a court may decide that a defendant had not been prejudiced since the evidence to be gathered close to the time of the incident is likely to have been the same.

Chapter 3—Evidence

3.01 *Generally.* In accordance with what has now become normal practice, the Criminal Procedure Rules 2015 (SI 2015/1490) replaced the 2014 rules with effect from October 5, 2015. The Criminal Procedure (Amendment) Rules 2016 (SI 2016/120) came into force on the April 4, 2016. The 2015 Rules were further amended by SI 2016/705 with effect from October 3, 2016: Criminal Procedure (Amendment No.2) Rules 2016. A main change in the Amendment No.2 Rules is the removal of the word "written" in a number of places related to the provision of notices; this reflects the move towards greater use of electronic transmission of information.

The Criminal Practice Directions 2015 ([2015] EWCA Crim 1567) replace the previous directions made on October 7, 2013, although annexes D and E to the Consolidated Criminal Practice Direction of July 8, 2002 (as amended) remain in force. They have been amended with effect from April 4, 2016, but those amendments do not affect this work: [2016] EWCA Crim 97.

3.32a *Relevance of good character.* In *R. v Hunter* [2015] EWCA Crim 631, the Court of Appeal reviewed a number of decisions with regard to the relevance of good character and the directions required. The court felt that the good character principles had been taken too far.

The court stated the following general principles:

(a) The general rule is that a direction as to the relevance of good character to a defendant's credibility is to be given where a defendant has a good character and either has testified or made pre-trial statements.

(b) The general rule is that a direction as to the relevance of a good character to the likelihood of a defendant having committed the offence charged is to be given where a defendant has a good character whether or not he testified or made pre-trial answers or statements.

(c) Where defendant A, of good character, is tried jointly with B who does not have a good character, (a) and (b) still apply.

(d) There are exceptions to the general rule, for example where a defendant has no previous convictions but has admitted other reprehensible conduct and the judge considers it would be an insult to common sense to give directions, in accordance with *R. v Vye* [1993] 1 WLR 47. The judge then has a residual discretion to decline to give a good character direction.

(e) A jury must not be misled.

(f) A judge is not obliged to give absurd or meaningless directions.

The court offered guidance as to the future approach to be adopted, identifying the following categories relating to good character:

(a) Absolute good character—D, having no previous convictions or cautions recorded against him and no other reprehensible conduct alleged, admitted or proven, is entitled to both limbs of the good character direction. The weight to be given to each limb is a matter for the jury.

(b) Effective good character—Where D has previous convictions or cautions recorded which are old, minor and have no relevance to the charge, the judge has to decide whether or not to treat D as a person of "effective good character". If the judge decides to treat D as a person of effective good character, the judge does not have discretion whether to give the direction. Both limbs of the direction must be given, modified as necessary to reflect the other matters and to thereby ensure that the jury is not mislead.

(c) Previous convictions/cautions adduced under s.101(1) (b) CJA2003 by the defence—D has no entitlement to either limb of the good character direction. It is a matter for the judge's discretion. The discretion is a broad one of the "open textured variety" whether to give any part of the direction and, if so, in what terms. It is not narrowly circumscribed.

(d) Bad character adduced under s.101 CJA 2003 and relied upon by the prosecution—The judge must give a bad character direction. There is discretion as to a good character direction, but if the evidence is of conviction or caution, it is difficult to envisage a good character direction that would not offend the absurdity principle.

(e) Bad character adduced by the defence under s.101 and not relied upon by the prosecution—D has no entitlement to either limb of the good character direction. It is a matter for the judge's discretion.

Evidence by the defendant. In *R. v Alfie Good* [2016] EWCA Crim 1054, a **3.38** defendant's conviction was upheld where he had failed to give evidence, he maintained, on the advice of his Counsel.

The defendant had assaulted a taxi driver but was advancing self-defence. The complainant gave evidence and self-defence was put to him under cross-examination. After receiving advice from his counsel and considering the matter overnight, the defendant elected not to give evidence. The recorder had asked the appropriate question of the defendant about adverse inferences before then quite properly directing the jury.

The Court of Appeal went as far as hearing from trial Counsel who maintained that he had given the proper advice in ordinary terms, but had not got his brief signed at the time, and the original brief was now missing.

The Court took the view that, although the advice had not been clear enough, the conviction was safe and the jury had properly been left to take an adverse inference from the failure to give evidence.

Documentary evidence: Certificates. In *Crader v Chief Constable of Hampshire* **3.51** [2015] EWHC 3553 (Admin), the Divisional Court held that magistrates had been entitled to treat a certificate under s.20 of the Road Traffic Offenders Act 1988, which had been signed by a prosecuting clerk, as issued in accordance with that section.

The defendant did not attend his trial, but argued on appeal that the magistrates had erred in law in relying upon the certificate as there was no evidence to support whether he had been authorised to sign the certificate.

The Divisional Court held that once it was clear that s.20(1) did not require a person who was authorised to say so in the certificate, then that implication could not be read in as a result of s.20(7). There were however indications on the face of the certificate that it emanated from the police, and was issued by a prosecuting clerk who was both cognisant with s.20 and satisfied of its requirements. Section 20(7) did not impliedly insert a further requirement.

3.67 *CCTV.* The Divisional Court has also recently considered the use of CCTV evidence in deciding whether justices were correct to dismiss a case on a submission of no case to answer in *DPP v Jobling*, unreported, May 26, 2016.

The defendant had been accused of damaging tyres on vehicles belonging to his neighbour. There was CCTV footage and officers and the complainant viewed this, whereupon the complainant immediately identified the defendant whom he had known for years. The magistrates dismissed the case on a submission finding that the CCTV evidence was of such poor quality that the defendant could not be identified from it, together with problems with breaches of Code D of the Police and Criminal Evidence Act 1984.

The Court held that the CCTV evidence went some way to establishing a prima facie case, and with the evidence taken as a whole, there was sufficient evidence to proceed. Conviction may be another matter and that was where the weight of the breaches of Code D and other factors could be considered. The magistrates had conflated no case to answer with conviction.

3.82 *Proof generally: Adverse inference and need to hold an identity parade.* The issue of whether an identification parade was required in a speeding case was discussed in *Bates v Crown Prosecution Service* [2015] EWHC 2346 (Admin). Here the defendant was stopped after being detected speeding by a police officer. The driver gave the defendant's name, address and date of birth, and produced a driving licence confirming those details. Three months before the trial, the defendant's solicitors indicated that identification was in issue—the defendant did not attend the trial, but his solicitors did. The magistrates convicted him and the issue on appeal was whether an identification parade was required under the PACE codes of practice, Code D para.3.12, as the officer was an eyewitness whose evidence was disputed. In dismissing the appeal, the Divisional Court held that there had been sufficient evidence upon which the court was entitled to convict.

The magistrates had been able to convict without drawing an adverse inference

Evidence

from the failure to give evidence. The officer was not an eyewitness who had identified a suspect within the meaning of para.3.12—he had seen the offence being committed and was merely reporting having been told by the driver that his name and address were those of the defendant. There was also nothing to suggest that the officer expressed an ability to identify the suspect within the meaning of para.3.12(ii). Neither of the two requirements for holding an identity parade were made out.

Chapter 4—Drink/Driving Offences

Definitions

4.31 *"Mechanically propelled vehicle": Whether disability scooter is a motor vehicle.* In *Croitoru v CPS* [2016] EWHC 1645 (Admin), a defendant had been convicted of driving a motor vehicle with excess alcohol when he was driving a mobility scooter that he had bought for his elderly father. He told the police that he had fitted it with a battery and was test driving it to see how far it would go. He was three times over the alcohol limit.

The issue on appeal was whether he could be convicted under s.5 of the Road Traffic Act 1988 if he was using a carriage as provided for under the Chronically Sick and Disabled Persons Act 1970.

Section 185 of the 1988 Act provides that a mechanically propelled invalid carriage, which complied with the prescribed requirements and was used in accordance with the prescribed conditions, was not to be treated as a motor vehicle for the purpose of ss 1 to 4 of the 1988 Act. There is no mention of s.5.

As there was no evidence that the scooter had been fitted with a new battery, and its use could not therefore be seen as transportation by a person other than the user to or from a place where maintenance had been carried out (reg.4(a) (ii) of the Use of Invalid Carriages on Highways Regulations 1988), then s.20 did not apply and therefore the scooter could be regarded as a motor vehicle.

4.270 *Reasonable excuse.* In *R. on the application of Cuns v Hammersmith Magistrates' Court* [2016] EWHC 748 (Admin), the administrative court considered the burden on the prosecution in disproving a reasonable excuse offered by a defendant facing a charge under s.7 of the Road Traffic Act 1988.

The case came before the Court on an application for judicial review following the refusal of the Justices to state a case. The case was rolled up so that the issue in the case was also considered, namely whether the magistrates had applied the wrong burden or reached an unreasonable conclusion in relation to the reasonableness of the reason given for not supplying a specimen of blood.

The defendant had refused to give a sample of blood and had claimed at the police station that he had a needle phobia.

The law is clear that it is for the Crown to prove that there was no reasonable excuse, but that does not mean that they have to discover reasonable excuses and then set about disproving them. They are only required to disprove a reasonable excuse if there is some evidential basis provided by the defendant that the issue is in play. The evidence of the doctor who took the sample was not available on the day of trial before the Justices, but the trial proceeded with the only evidence of the needle phobia being what the defendant had said to the police. No medical evidence was called for the defendant and he declined to give evidence about his phobia or about the circumstances at the police station.

The administrative court ruled that merely asserting at the police station the presence of a needle phobia was not sufficient. There had to be some evidence before the magistrates' court that then requires the Crown to disprove it.

The Justices had therefore been correct in refusing to state a case as they had not made any error of law in their findings.

Procedure and trial. In the recent first instance case of *R. v Cipriani* the Chief **4.324** Magistrate and Senior District Judge, Howard Riddle, convicted the defendant of driving a motor vehicle with excess alcohol.

As a first instance hearing this is not a binding authority and the conviction probably turns on its material facts and may yet be subject to appeal.

In the course of his 18-page judgement delivered on the June 24, 2016, the Chief Magistrate has alluded to issues that can commonly arise in drink drive cases and has attempted to issue some general guidance for all those involved in such cases.

It is hoped that, by producing those guidelines here, this can provide a useful framework both for lawyers and courts in preparing for the trial of such offences. With his permission that guidance is detailed below.

"Case Management at the First Hearing

It is essential that the real issues in the case be identified at the first hearing. If no issues are raised, or if the Crown is put to proof, it would normally be inappropriate to trouble prosecution witnesses to attend court. The trial can be put down for proof on the statements (either by Section 9 MCA or under Section 114 CJA 2003, interests of justice).

  (a) It is insufficient to refer to the 'reliability of breath alcohol readings'. The nature of the unreliability needs to be identified. If it is radio interference, that must be made clear. Similarly, if the question is calibration then that should be made clear. If the issue is that the operator failed to detect an error on the face of the print out, then that should be made clear.

  (b) If the issue is that the statutory warning has not been given, then this should be spelled out in the case management form (and later dealt with in cross-examination).

  (c) If the issue is *Cracknell v Willis* then the defendant would be expected at the first hearing to indicate what he had to drink and when during the relevant period. That is so that the Crown can check with their own expert, if they wish.

Expert Witnesses

Experts will be expected to attend the hearing and give evidence. It can be assumed that the court will require this. The procedure is covered by the Criminal Procedure Rules, and the Criminal Practice Directions Part 19 A.2. The expert evidence must be served on the Crown but this does not bypass the need for them to attend court unless the Court specifically otherwise agrees.

As a separate point, serving Section 9 statements that are likely to be contentious should be avoided, and it should not be assumed that the court will allow such statements to be read unless the CPS has signalled its agreement in writing.

Disclosure

The court should not be troubled with disclosure arguments on the day of trial. These should be resolved in advance, by way of a Section 8 application if appropriate. It is a matter for the prosecutor (not the defence) to apply for an adjournment to comply with this obligation and (absent a Section 8 CPIA application) it is for the prosecutor (not the court) to decide whether disclosure has been dealt with.

Record of the Hearing

A magistrates' court is not a court of record. Ultimately the parties must accept the decision of the court as to what evidence was or was not given. If an expert is to be asked about evidence given by prosecution witnesses, the normal and better approach is for that expert to attend and hear the evidence directly. To proceed by putting an incomplete and potentially inaccurate statement to the expert witness is of little or no value to the court. It is usually unhelpful for an advocate to attempt to introduce into the evidence his notes, or other people's notes, where he knows the court has a different understanding of the evidence (unless invited to do so by the court).

Neither counsel's notes nor the legal adviser's notes can be used in any appeal to the Crown Court.

Reliability of the EBM

Where you are asking the court not to accept the reading provided by the EBM then advocates are under a professional duty to remind the court that there is a presumption that the EBM is working accurately. They must quote the following passage from Lord Griffiths in *Cracknell v Willis*:

'I am myself hopeful that the good sense of the magistrates and that the realisation by the motoring public that approved breath testing machines are proving reliable will combine to ensure that few defendants will seek to challenge a breath analysis by spurious evidence of their consumption of alcohol. The magistrates will remember that the presumption in law is that the machine is reliable.'

They should also remind the bench of the assumption that the proportion of alcohol in the specimen of breath at the time of the offence was not less than in the specimen.

Both the assumption and the presumption are rebuttable.

Calibration

In any case where advocates assert that the Crown must produce evidence of calibration they have a professional obligation to provide the following dicta from Sullivan J in *Haggis*:

'In simple terms, there was evidence in that case [*Mayon*] that there was or might have been a problem with the machine. There was no such evidence in the present case. There was nothing to gainsay PC Fagin's evidence that it was "working properly".

Mr Ley accepts that had that been the sum total of her evidence it might have been reasonable to infer that a machine that was "working properly" was correctly calibrating itself. He submits that PC Fagin's answer in cross-examination that she did not know the calibration limits of the machine means that she could not have know whether it had correctly calibrated itself and therefore could not have known whether it was working properly.

As I have indicated, when considering the answer to question 2, beyond eliciting the fact that PC Fagin did not know the correct calibration limits of the machine, there was no attempt to challenge her evidence that the machine was working properly, that it had produced a print out and that the readings at least appeared to PC Fagin (accepting that she did not know the calibration limits) to be appropriate and that the lowest reading was 43 microgrammes in 10 millilitres of breath.

The appellant had been provided with a copy of the print out. If there was anything in the print out (which was not produced to the judge) to indicate that the machine was not working properly that could, and no doubt would, have been put to PC Fagin in cross examination. In these circumstances, and each case will turn very much upon its own particular facts, the judge was entitled to conclude:

> "That there was no evidence at all which would have raised any doubt about the question as to whether the machine was operating correctly."

Since it is "well known" that the machine tests itself, I do not accept that the prosecution have to prove that this is characteristic of the machine on each and every occasion. It may be taken that the device does test itself unless there is something to indicate that it might not have done so in the particular circumstances of the case. Pausing there, there was evidence in this case that this machine did test itself, that is to say that it was self calibrating. Although the operator's knowledge was imperfect, her evidence was, nevertheless, that the machine in her view was working properly and nothing was put to her suggest that her evidence in this respect was or might have been wrong.'"

Chapter 5—Dangerous, Careless and Inconsiderate Driving, etc.

Causing Death by Driving: Unlicensed, Disqualified or Uninsured Drivers

5.101 *Causing death by careless, or inconsiderate, driving.* The issue of causation in the offence of causing death by careless driving was considered by the Court of Appeal on March 22, 2016 in *R. v Sutton (Roger)* [2016] EWCA Crim 540.

The defendant had set up his own company as a private ambulance and had his own transit van adapted to take wheelchairs and stretchers. He did not purport to provide any medical care. He was asked to transport an 85-year-old lady from her home to hospital. A collision occurred whereby the victim came out of her wheelchair and struck her head. She subsequently went into cardiac arrest and died. The case was that he had not left sufficient distance to the vehicle in front and had therefore driven carelessly and that the injury suffered in that collision had caused the cardiac arrest and was the real cause of her death. He also faced a health and safety prosecution as she was not properly restrained in a three-point safety belt.

The sole issue for the appeal was that of causation and whether there was sufficient evidence that the accident was the cause of death. The medical evidence was that the victim had severe coronary heart disease and was vulnerable to sudden abnormality of the heart rhythm which would lead to a cardiac arrest. The doctor also went on to confirm that in his opinion the temporal relationship between the incident and the collapse was clear, although cautioning that an individual such as this would always be at risk of sudden death at any time.

The trial judge rejected a submission of no case to answer and later refused a further adjournment to allow the prosecution to rebut evidence of a defence expert. This was, in the view of the appeal court, entirely within his case management powers. The appeal court was satisfied that the conviction was safe and the trial judge had been correct not to withdraw the case from the jury.

5.103 *Causing death by driving.* The Supreme Court has considered whether the words "owing to the driving of the vehicle" imported an element of mens rea to the offence of aggravated vehicle taking: *R. v Taylor* [2016] UKSC 5; [2016] 1 W.L.R. 500. See note to § 15.31, below in this supplement.

Sentencing Guidelines

5.140 The Court of Appeal (Criminal Division) further reviewed sentencing for the offence of causing death by careless driving on June 22, 2016 in *R. v Ubbey (Harvinder)* [2016] EWCA Crim 809.

An 89-year-old man had been crossing the road when he was struck by the defendant who was driving a powerful car. He had been seen driving fast and aggressively, tailgating and undertaking vehicles and, at the time of the accident, was travelling at between 31 to 41mph in a road restricted to 30mph. He had been charged with causing death by dangerous driving but was convicted of the lesser offence. The judge put the offence in category 1A of the sentencing guidelines, which had a starting point of 15 months. The defendant was a man of previous good character and did not have a driving record.

The judge had passed a sentence of 30 months which was twice the length of the starting point, and had failed to give sufficient weight to his good character and the impact of the conviction upon him and his family. The sentence was reduced to two years' imprisonment.

In *R. v Usaceva (Marina)* [2015] EWCA Crim 166, a six-year sentence following a guilty plea to causing death by dangerous driving was held not to be excessive. The victim's car had been struck from behind by the defendant's car and spun across the road into the path of an articulated lorry. Minutes before the crash, the defendant had been using two mobile phones, and there was no other explanation as to why she was unable to stop. She had two previous convictions for using a mobile phone whilst driving. She had lied to the police and tried to conceal the phones. She also declined the judge's invitation to give evidence following her guilty plea about the cause of the accident and use of the phones. The judge put the offence in category two as it involved driving in a way that created a substantial risk of danger, then increased it by two years for the previous convictions and reduced it by one year for the guilty plea. However, the judge had been wrong to both disqualify and impose 11 penalty points.   **5.143**

In *R. v Shanmugarasa Vinayagasivampillai* [2015] EWCA Crim 1769, a sentence of four years imprisonment for causing death by dangerous driving was reduced to three years on appeal. The defendant was driving his uncle's van after completing a 12-hour shift the night before. He had gone home but his uncle had asked him to go to the cash and carry. On driving back to his uncle's shop, the van veered across the road and collided with the victim who was jogging along the road. The victim had a 21-month-old daughter and her death had a devastating effect on her family. The defendant kept falling asleep once detained. The judge said that the defendant was not someone with any intention of causing harm to anyone, but he should not have been anywhere near a motor car. He placed the offence within level 3, with a starting point of three years and a range to two to five years. As aggravating factors, the judge noted the defendant's poor driving record and previous convictions for excess alcohol and for driving whilst disqualified. With full credit for guilty plea, the sentence was four years imprisonment and a six-year driving disqualification. However, the Court of Appeal decided that the starting point should be four and a half years as there were points of mitigation, such as genuine remorse and the defendant's hard-working character. With full credit for plea, the sentence was thus reduced to three years.

The issue of the level of sentence on an offence of causing death by careless driving when under the influence of drink or drugs contrary to s.3A of the Road Traffic Act 1988 was considered by the Court of Appeal in *R. v Gareth David Entwhistle* [2016] EWCA Crim 487.

The sentence in question was one of five and a half years' imprisonment and a five-year disqualification from driving.

The defendant had pleaded guilty 14 days before the trial was due to take place. There was a head-on collision on a rural Welsh road. The victim, a 21-year-old student, had been driving home and was on the correct side of the road. The defendant had cut a corner and was on the wrong side of the road at the time of the collision and was estimated to have been driving at between 36 and 67mph. There was expert evidence that a vehicle could have safely negotiated that bend at up to 67mph, and the collision was therefore down to excessive speed or loss of control. The defendant had a blood alcohol reading of 132 millilitres, significantly over the prescribed limit of 80 in blood. There was evidence of similar poor driving from the defendant earlier in the day. The complainant died at the scene and the defendant was taken to hospital as he had suffered a serious orthopaedic injury.

The defendant told the police that he had no recollection of the accident and that he could not recall drinking.

The sentencing judge said that when the defendant set off he knew that he had been drinking and had had a substantial amount to drink. He had a short journey to make on a road he knew well and had no reason to drive so fast. He viewed the carelessness as falling into the most significant bracket allowing for the level of alcohol and the starting point was therefore six years, which after discount for the guilty plea would be a sentence of five years six months' imprisonment.

The appeal court found that the judge's choice of starting point could not be criticised. The drinking and the nature of the careless driving has to be taken in the round. This case clearly fell into the category of carelessness with the description of not short of dangerousness. The starting point was therefore appropriate. The Court took the view however that there had not been sufficient discount for the late guilty plea. The discount should have been between 10 per cent (that applicable on the day of trial) and 25 per cent. The witnesses had been saved the anxiety of attending court and the discount should have been 12 months which equated to a little under 17 per cent.

5.146   Sentencing for the offence of causing death by dangerous driving was again considered by the Court of Appeal on January 27, 2016 in *R. v Piotr Trojanowski* [2016] EWCA Crim 159.

The defendant had driven his articulated lorry into the rear of a Mercedes van, causing the death of its driver. The motorway had been restricted to 50mph and the lorry's tachograph showed the defendant to be driving at 56mph and that he did not brake until the last second if at all. He was convicted after trial and had told a witness at the scene that he thought he had fallen asleep. The judge sentenced him on the basis that he had fallen asleep whilst driving a 36-ton lorry, that he had passed a number of warning signs to which other drivers had responded correctly and that this was an aggravating feature. The case fell at the top end of level 3 of the guidelines meriting a sentence of four years six months, with a period of disqualification from driving of seven years together with an order for an extended retest.

The Appeal Court took the view that the period of disqualification for a professional driver was excessive and reduced it to five years.

Sentencing: Causing serious injury by dangerous driving. In *R. v Hussain* [2015] **5.147a** EWCA Crim 1016, the Court of Appeal again addressed the issue of sentencing for the offence of causing serious injury by dangerous driving. It held that a sentence of two years imprisonment was not manifestly excessive for a defendant who had a number of previous driving convictions and where the victim's injuries had been horrific. The disqualification was, however, reduced from seven to four years as the defendant was a taxi driver and his ability to drive would be important to his chances of obtaining employment. Whilst speeding, the defendant had attempted to beat the changing traffic lights at a pedestrian crossing and had collided with a pedestrian, causing horrific injuries. The defendant did not plead guilty until the day of the trial. It was accepted that, had the victim died, this would have been a level 3 offence.

The Court of Appeal took the opportunity to review the sentencing guidelines for this offence in *R. v Robert Smart* [2015] EWCA Crim 1756. The defendant was sentenced to two years imprisonment and a four-year driving disqualification, including an extended driving test requirement. The defendant was overtaking a slower vehicle when he collided head on with a motorcyclist travelling in the opposite direction. The victim was a 54-year-old farmer who suffered life-changing injuries, including an amputation of his left leg below the knee. The defendant had overtaken two vehicles, but this was a momentary misjudgement albeit with very serious consequences. It would appear that the sentencing judge was not referred to any of five cases that have been dealt with by the Court of Appeal, starting with *R. v Dewdney* [2015] (as outlined in the 27th edition) and ending with *R. v Hussain* (above). *Dewdney* established the principle that where there were no sentencing guidelines for this offence, the correct approach was to have regard to the guideline for causing death by dangerous driving.

In this case, the judge had taken a starting point of three years, which would have been the same had the victim been killed. The Court of Appeal viewed this as a level 3 offence in the dangerous driving guidelines—and, given the extensive mitigation, two years was the appropriate starting point. With a full one-third discount, this gave a sentence of 16 months. There were no compelling reasons to suspend the sentence.

The Court of Appeal Criminal Division again explored the sentencing level for the offence of causing serious injury by dangerous driving on February 18, 2016 in *R. v Howsego (Jason Patrick)* [2016] EWCA Crim 120.

The defendant had pleaded guilty to aggravated vehicle taking, causing serious injury by dangerous driving, together with no insurance and failing to stop after an accident. He was sentenced to 28 months' imprisonment for the offence of causing serious injury by dangerous driving, with a concurrent six months for the aggravated taking and no separate penalty for the other matters. He was also disqualified for six years and until an extended driving test was passed.

A head-on collision had occurred with the defendant driving a Mercedes at speed on the wrong side of the road when he collided with a transit van being driven in the opposite direction. The driver of the transit suffered serious injuries. The Mercedes had been taken during a burglary and had false plates. The defendant who had left the scene of the accident returned in drink some four hours later looking for his dog.

The appeal court concluded that the judge fell into error in her approach to the guidelines for causing death by dangerous driving. The appeal court referred to *R. v Dewdney* [2014] and *R. v Jenkins* [2015]. In those cases Treacy LJ had held that the headroom for this offence is relatively limited because of the relatively modest maximum sentence and the bands of sentencing are therefore compressed.

The judge therefore took too high a starting point as the correct starting point should have been three and a half years, and with full credit for a guilty plea the sentence should have been one of two years' imprisonment. Although a modest reduction, this is an effect of the compressed levels of sentencing for this offence.

The case of *R. v Sandhu (Gurpreet)* [2016] EWCA Crim 924, involved a similar offence and was considered by the Court of Appeal on March 23, 2016. Here the defendant had been driving at a speed of 60mph on a three-lane urban road and collided with a 91-year-old pedestrian. It was said that the defendant was late for work, and the offence was aggravated by very wet conditions and the fact that he had a previous conviction for dangerous driving. The pedestrian suffered serious injuries from which he appeared to recover, but died before the case was heard. It was made clear that the causal link could not be established to face the more serious charge. In sentencing the judge placed the offence in category 1 of the death by dangerous guidelines because of the excessive speed in adverse weather conditions, aggravated by his previous conviction and used a starting point of four years, which, with discount for guilty plea, gave a sentence of three years. He was disqualified from driving for seven years.

On appeal the court found that the facts more properly equated to the top of level 2, with the aggravating factors of the grossly excessive speed, the very wet road conditions, and the fact that the defendant knew the road and therefore would be well aware of the likelihood of pedestrians, together with his previous conviction. The sentence of three years, although deservedly severe, was not manifestly excessive. The appeal was allowed in part, with the disqualification being reduced to five years.

Dangerous, Careless and Inconsiderate Driving, etc.

The guidance in *Dewdney* was again considered by the Court of Appeal on April 8, 2016 in *R. v Shaw (Nicky Christopher)* [2016] EWCA Crim 805.

The defendant had, in a built up area, attempted to overtake a taxi in a 30mph limit. He could not return to his own carriageway due to a concrete pedestrian refuge and collided head on with a car travelling in the opposite direction. That driver sustained serious injuries and had to be cut free from his vehicle. The defendant had tried to say that his brakes were defective (which they were not) and that the injuries had been made worse as the other driver was not wearing a seatbelt. The sentencing judge used the guideline for death by dangerous driving and was not referred to any recent authorities to assist in sentencing.

The Court in reviewing sentence again referred to *Dewdney*, and other subsequent cases all of which are said to turn on own their own facts.

Here, there were factors which could put the offence in level 3; there was the speed that was inappropriate for the prevailing conditions; a brief but obvious danger; and the distraction of loud music. Because of the combination of factors this was a group of determinants which would lift the offence into level 2.

In equating this finding of a dangerous act resulting in serious injury, the court then had to consider the compressed scale and the lack of guidelines. The Court had regard to s.143(1) of the Criminal Justice Act 2003, which states:

> "In considering the seriousness of any offence, the court must consider the offenders culpability in committing the offence and any harm which the offence caused, was intended to cause or might foreseeably have caused".

The Court agreed that the correct starting point was three years, with full credit for plea resulting in two years. The appeal against sentence was therefore dismissed.

Finally on April 22, 2016 the Court of Appeal again referred to the problem in sentencing such cases in *R. v Taylor (Andrew Philip)*, unreported.

The defendant had purchased, for £50, a cheap but powerful motorcycle and rode it around a residential estate with a series of pillion passengers. He hit a 15-year-old boy who was playing football whilst travelling at between 50 to 60mph. He suffered serious life-changing injuries. He later assaulted another male and was charged also with causing grievous bodily harm.

Again the sentencing judge's attention had not been drawn to *Dewdney* and other relevant sentencing cases. The sentence of three years and four months (40 months) was reduced to 31 months on appeal.

Dangerous and careless driving: Sentencing. The Court of Appeal reviewed the **5.150** length of a custodial sentence given for dangerous driving in *R. v Mindaugas Baublys* [2015] EWCA Crim 1411. The defendant was a Lithuanian national working as a delivery driver, who had collided head on with another vehicle while carrying out a dangerous overtaking manoeuvre on the winding Snake Pass. The driver of the oncoming car and her passenger were injured, as was the driver of a following car. The injuries were not serious, but did have emotional and financial consequences for the victims.

During sentencing, the judge described it as an astonishingly stupid piece of driving—overtaking on a blind bend in the dark, in damp conditions with a high likelihood of a collision. He acknowledged that the defendant was a young man of good character with a good work record, but said that his starting point after trial would have been 18 months. The judge gave credit for the guilty plea and personal mitigation, and arrived at eight months imprisonment. The sentence was reduced to six months on appeal, using a starting point of nine months after trial with a full one-third reduction for guilty plea.

A further example of sentencing for dangerous driving is provided by *R. v Hamlett* [2015] EWCA Crim 1412, where the issue was the use of a deprivation order. The defendant pleaded guilty to dangerous driving and was sentenced to a 12-month suspended sentence—with 240 hours unpaid work, a two-year disqualification and an order made under s.143 of the Powers of Criminal Courts (Sentencing) Act 2000, to deprive him of the motor vehicle involved. The question was whether that order should stand, as there had been no proper investigation of the vehicle's value or the impact of deprivation as required by s.143(5).

The defendant had been driving between 70 and 90mph through red lights in an area restricted to 30mph. He had crashed into a tree whilst being chased by the police. The appeal was allowed, in that the Crown had to put some evidence before the judge before an order was made (*R. v Pemberton* [1982]). The order appeared to have been an afterthought by the judge when prompted by the Crown, as he had not referred to the possible order in his sentencing remarks. The order, equating to a further financial penalty of £10,000 (the value of the car), was manifestly excessive.

Chapter 6—Driver Offences

Signs and Signals

Generally. The Traffic Signs Regulations and General Directions 2016 (SI 2016/ **6.01**
362) came into force on April 22, 2016.

The Regulations are reproduced in the later parts of this supplement to volume 2.

The rules determine what traffic signs should look like, what they mean and how they may be placed and illuminated.

The aim is to provide a less prescriptive set of regulations, allowing traffic authorities greater flexibility to develop signing schemes that meet local needs, whilst safeguarding national consistency.

There are two parts:

> Part 1: The Traffic Signs Regulations 2016, and
> Part 2: The Traffic Signs General Directions 2016.

The aim is to make the instrument easier to navigate, with all provisions about a particular sign in the same schedule.

Generally, the meaning and design of a sign is set out in a table in a schedule and that table then identifies which other provisions (both regulations and general directions) elsewhere in the schedule are applicable to that sign.

The regulations are designed both to update and consolidate, and as a result replace the following regulations:

- the Zebra, Pelican and Puffin Crossing Regulations and General Directions 1997 (as amended);
- the Traffic Signs (Temporary Obstructions) Regulations 1997;
- the Traffic Signs Regulations and General Directions Regulations 2002 (as amended);
- the School Crossing Patrol Sign (England and Wales) Regulations 2006.

An example of how the Schedules are put together can be found by using Schedule 10, relevant for this chapter as it deals with signs for speed limits.

> Part 1: deals with provisions applying to signs in Part 2.
> Part 2: Contains a table of signs with nine diagrams of signs, their sizing and detail, including the degree of flexibility.
> Part 3: details the provisions applying to signs in Part 2.
> Part 4: gives the general directions.

The full list of schedules is provided below to assist in finding the appropriate references.

Schedule 1: Definitions

Schedule 2: Signs that warn of hazards and signs for bridges and other structures.

Schedule 3: Upright signs that indicate regulatory requirements for moving traffic.

Schedule 4: Upright signs that control waiting, loading and parking along a road.

Schedule 5: Signs to indicate parking places and areas subject to parking controls.

Schedule 6: Upright signs for red routes.

Schedule 7: Road markings and miscellaneous upright signs that indicate stopping, waiting, loading and parking controls.

Schedule 8: Signs indicating the entrance to and the end of a pedestrian, or pedestrian cycle zone, and signs for charging schemes.

Schedule 9: Regulatory signs at junctions and miscellaneous regulatory signs.

Schedule 10: Signs for speed limits.

Schedule 11: Signs that give information, are advisory or guide traffic.

Schedule 12: Directional signs.

Schedule 13: Signs only for use in temporary situations.

Schedule 14: Signs for traffic control by light signals, signs for crossings, and signs for lane control.

Schedule 15: Matrix signs and light signals for the control of moving traffic on motorways and all-purpose dual carriageway roads.

Schedule 16: Variable message signs.

Schedule 17: Letters, numerals and other characters.

Schedule 18: Permitted Expressions of Time, Distance and Parking Restrictions.

Schedule 19: Revocations.

Speed Limits

6.80   *Evidence and corroboration: Issue of identity in speeding.* The issue of whether an identification parade was required in a speeding case was discussed in *Bates v Crown Prosecution Service* [2015] EWHC 2346 (Admin). Here the defendant was stopped after being detected speeding by a police officer. The driver gave the defendant's name, address and date of birth, and produced a driving licence confirming those details. Three months before the trial, the defendant's solicitors indicated that identification was in issue—the defendant did not attend the trial, but his solicitors did. The magistrates convicted him and the issue on appeal was whether an identification parade was required under the PACE codes of practice, Code D para.3.12, as the officer was an eyewitness whose evidence was disputed.

In dismissing the appeal, the Divisional Court held that there had been sufficient evidence upon which the court was entitled to convict.

The magistrates had been able to convict without drawing an adverse inference from the failure to give evidence. The officer was not an eyewitness who had identified a suspect within the meaning of para.3.12—he had seen the offence being committed and was merely reporting having been told by the driver that his name and address were those of the defendant. There was also nothing to suggest that the officer expressed an ability to identify the suspect within the meaning of para.3.12(ii). Neither of the two requirements for holding an identity parade were made out.

Evidence generally: Certificates. In *Crader v Chief Constable of Hampshire*　**6.101** [2015] EWHC 3553 (Admin), the Divisional Court held that magistrates had been entitled to treat a certificate under s.20 of the Road Traffic Offenders Act 1988, which had been signed by a prosecuting clerk, as issued in accordance with that section.

The defendant did not attend his trial, but argued on appeal that the magistrates had erred in law in relying upon the certificate as there was no evidence to support whether he had been authorised to sign the certificate.

The Divisional Court held that once it was clear that s.20(1) did not require a person who was authorised to say so in the certificate, then that implication could not be read in as a result of s.20(7). There were however indications on the face of the certificate that it emanated from the police, and was issued by a prosecuting clerk who was both cognisant with s.20 and satisfied of its requirements. Section 20(7) did not impliedly insert a further requirement.

Chapter 7—Accidents Involving Injury

7.01   *Generally.* In accordance with what has now become normal practice, the Criminal Procedure Rules 2015 (SI 2015/1490) (as amended) have replaced the Criminal Procedure Rules 2014 (SI 2014/1610). The 2015 Rules came into effect on October 5, 2015 and were amended by SI 2016/120 with effect from April 4, 2016: Criminal Procedure (Amendment) Rules 2016 and by SI 2016/705 with effect from October 3, 2016: Criminal Procedure (Amendment No.2) Rules 2016. The rules were accompanied by new Criminal Practice Directions 2015 [2015] EWCA 1567 (as amended with effect from April 4, 2016: [2016] EWCA Crim 97). Few of the changes that have been made affect the rules or the directions referred to in the main work. Accordingly, unless specifically mentioned in this supplement, the number and content of the rules described in the main work remain the same. A main change in the Amendment No.2 Rules is the removal of the word "written" in a number of places related to the provision of notices; this reflects the move towards greater use of electronic transmission of information.

Chapter 10—Insurance

Third Party Insurance Policies

Nature of the insurance. A further issue has arisen regarding the extent to which **10.05** a policy of insurance can contain limitations on the extent of cover provided. In *Litaska UAB v BTA Insurance Co. SE* [2015] R.T.R. 21, a Lithuanian road haulage company had insurance which required notification and payment of a supplement in order to use an insured motor vehicle outside the country for a specified period. An accident occurred in the UK; the insurance company met the claims of the victim, but subsequently sought to recover part of that from the insured and was successful in the national courts. On appeal to the European Court of Justice, it was held that the limitation was invalid. Article 2 of Directive 90/232 requires all compulsory insurance policies to provide cover on the basis of a single premium through the entire territory of the EU for the whole length of the policy, and it was not acceptable to place an additional requirement of notification and payment of a supplement on the insured.

Void conditions. See note to § 10.05, above in this supplement. **10.28**

Proceedings and Penalties

Exclusion from liability – vehicle used in the furtherance of crime. Reference is **10.81** made in the main work to the decision in *Delaney v Pickett* [2011] EWCA Civ 1532, in which the Court of Appeal upheld a decision to reject a claim against the MIB where the passenger and driver had both been in possession of substantial amounts of cannabis. In the course of the judgment, the Court of Appeal noted that the claimant had sought to raise the extent to which the Uninsured Drivers Agreement was compatible with the appropriate EU Directive, but the argument had been raised too late for consideration. However, the issue was subsequently brought before the court and is reported as *Delaney v Secretary of State for Transport* [2015] EWCA Civ 172; [2015] R.T.R. 19. At first instance, the court upheld the decision that the provisions in cl.6.1(e) were incompatible with the provisions of Directive 84/5 and, therefore, the United Kingdom was in breach of its obligations under EU law. Compensation was ordered as a result.

Following this decision, a new agreement has been published which affects all accidents occurring on or after August 1, 2015. The exemption replacing cl. 6.1(e) is now contained in cl.8, and limits the exemption to those who

"knew or had reason to believe that—
(a) the vehicle had been stolen or unlawfully taken; or

(b) the vehicle was being used without therebeing in force in relation to its use a contract of insurance complying with Part VI of the 1988 Act."

The full text of the agreement is available at *https://www.mib.org.uk/media/166917/2015-uninsured-drivers-agreement-england-scotland-wales.pdf* (Accessed April 12, 2016).

Chapter 11—Driving Licences

Provisions and Offences

Generally. The Motor Vehicles (Driving Licences) (Amendment) (No. 4) **11.07**
Regulations 2015 (SI 2015/1797), came into force on December 31, 2015. They
amend the 1999 Regulations in relation to tests of competence to drive—they
recognise that anyone presenting himself for a manoeuvres test, or for a practical
test for particular classes of vehicle, may satisfy the examiner of the statutory
requirements by producing either certificates of completion of approved training
courses or a "manoeuvres test pass certificate" by production of the Northern
Ireland equivalent. There is a similar provision relating to drivers who have a
licence to drive cars who are able to produce a Northern Ireland equivalent of a
valid certificate of completion of an approved training course for motor cyclists.

Regulations 9 and 10 of the 2015 Regulations partly implement the Commission Directive 2014/85/EU which amends Directive 2006/126/EC on driving
licences. The words "safe driving in road tunnels" is included in the list of specified matters which a candidate may be tested on in the theory test, whilst reg.10
implements para.1(c) to (e) of the Annex to the Directive by adding more items to
the list of specified requirements, in relation to behaviour in traffic, which a
candidate may be tested on in the practical or unitary test.

Exchangeable driving licences. The Driving Licences (Exchangeable Licences) **11.69**
Order 2016 (SI 2016/277) designates Switzerland as making satisfactory provision for the issue of certain classes of driving licence, thus enabling a person
holding one of those licences to exchange it for a corresponding British licence.
The licences affected are those issued in Switzerland which authorise the driving
of large goods vehicles and large buses (with or without a trailer). The Order
provides that a Swiss licence authorising the driving of vehicles with automatic
transmission is exchangeable for a British licence authorising the driving of
vehicles with automatic transmission only. The Order took effect on March 23,
2016.

Chapter 12—Excise and Trade Licences

Rates of Duty

12.09   *Rates of Duty.*   It should be noted that on July 8, 2015, HM Revenue and Customs published a policy paper on vehicle excise duty. The measure will reform vehicle excise duty for cars registered from April 1, 2017 onwards. First Year Rates of vehicle excise duty will vary according to the carbon dioxide emissions of the vehicle. A flat standard rate of £140 will apply in all subsequent years—except for zero-emission cars, for which the standard rate will be £0. Cars with a list price above £40,000 will attract a supplement of £310 on their standard rate for the first five years in which such a rate is paid. All cars first registered before April 1, 2017 will remain in the current vehicle excise duty system. (See *https:// www.gov.uk/government/publications/vehicle-excise-duty* (Accessed April 12, 2016).)

Chapter 13—Goods and Passenger Vehicles

Certificates of professional competence. The Vehicle Drivers (Certificates of **13.06**
Professional Competence) (Amendment) Regulations 2015 (SI 2015/2024), came
into force on January 25, 2016. They amend the 2007 Regulations, which require
drivers of lorries, buses and coaches to obtain a qualification entitled a Driver
"Certificate of Professional Competence" (CPC) and to undergo 35 hours of
training every five years.

Apart from deleting references to "the Driving Licences Directive", the
Regulations update references to that Directive by substituting a reference to the
Motor Vehicles (Driving Licences) Regulations 1999 for Great Britain, and a
similar provision relating to Northern Ireland.

The main practical application of the 2015 Regulations is to amend and extend
the radius within which an empty goods or passenger vehicle can be driven from
the place where a driver is based without the driver requiring a Driver CPC. The
radius is extended from 50km to 100km. The 50km radius was originally
designed to align with the EU drivers' hours tachograph regulation for vehicles
which carried materials, equipment or machinery for the use of the driver in the
course of his work. That relaxation was amended to 100km in 2015 by virtue of
amendments to EU Regulation 561/2006, as inserted by Regulation EU 165/
2014.

Other changes introduced by the 2015 Regulations include the addition of the
Prison Service to the existing list of bodies which are exempt from the application of the requirement for drivers to hold a Driver CPC.

Chapter 14—Drivers' Hours and Records

Drivers' Hours: Goods Vehicles

14.67   Amendments to the Drivers' Hours Rules took effect on March 2, 2015 by virtue of art.45 of Regulation (EU) No. 165/2014 on tachographs in road transport, which amended art.3 (exemptions) and art.13 (national derogations) of Regulation (EC) 561/2006 on Drivers' Hours. A directly applicable exemption was introduced for vehicles or combinations of vehicles with a maximum permissible mass not exceeding 7.5 tonnes used for carrying materials, equipment or machinery for the driver's use in the course of his work, and which are used only within a 100km radius from the base of the undertaking on condition that driving the vehicle does not constitute the driver's main activity. Certain national derogations were also widened with effect from March 2, 2015.

14.131   Regulation (EU) No. 165/2014 deals with tachographs in road transport and repeals Council Regulation (EEC) No. 3821/85 on recording equipment in road transport. It further amends Regulation (EC) No. 561/2006 on the harmonisation of certain social legislation relating to road transport. The new Regulation is designed to tackle fraud by making the tachograph more resistant to tampering and to facilitate enforcement. One of its aims is to reduce administrative burdens and standards for workshops. The regulations are strengthened in relation to the requirement to install, check, inspect and repair the tachograph. Some of the exemptions and derogations set out in the EU Drivers' Hours Rules are extended (see § 14.67, above). A number of changes took effect on March 2, 2015 relating to the approval of workshops, fitters and vehicle manufacturers.

New technical specifications are set out in the Regulations, thus providing for a new generation tachograph which will include connection to global navigation satellite systems. A harmonised interface is proposed in order that Intelligent Transport Systems may be used with the tachograph.

In order to update the legislative framework by the implementation date of March 2, 2016, domestic legislation has been updated.

14.132   There are various provisions in the 2014 Regulation relating to the retrofitting of vehicles travelling abroad (art.3(4)), tachograph security (art.20), inspections of tachographs (art.23) and tachograph offences (art.32). There are also provisions for the use of control officers and remote detection of tachograph offences.

14.149   Article 33.3 of the 2014 Regulation imposes upon transport undertakings liability for infringements of the new regulation which are committed by their drivers or by drivers who are at their disposal. There is an option to make operators' liability for drivers' infringements conditional upon their having failed to comply with one or more of their duties set out in either art.33.1 or art.10(1) and 10(2) of EU Regulation 561/2006.

Chapter 15—Theft, Taking Conveyances, Aggravated Vehicle-taking, Criminal Damage and Causing Danger to Road Users

Aggravated Vehicle-Taking

15.31 *The offence (Theft Act 1968, s.12A).* The Supreme Court has considered whether the words "owing to the driving of the vehicle" imported an element of mens rea to the offence of aggravated vehicle taking: *R. v Taylor* [2016] EWCA Crim 829; [2016] 1 W.L.R. 500. The driver of a scooter had been killed in an accident when the appellant had been driving a truck he had taken without the owner's consent. Although the appellant was over the drink drive limit, there was no evidence to suggest his driving was at fault. Nevertheless, relying on *R. v Marsh* [1997] R.T.R. 195, the Crown maintained the appellant was guilty of aggravated vehicle-taking. The Court of Appeal had ruled in *Marsh* that fault was not an element of an offence under s.12A of the Theft Act 1968. Laws J had held that the prosecution need only prove that an accident had occurred whilst a vehicle had been taken without consent, and not that the accident occurred because of the manner in which the accused had driven the vehicle.

The Supreme Court considered the case of *Hughes* [2013] UKSC 56; [2013] R.T.R. 31 (see § 5.103 of the main work). In that case, the Supreme Court had found that a conviction for an offence of "causing" death by driving whilst uninsured (under s.3ZB of the Road Traffic Act 1988) requires proof that the defendant's driving "involves some element of fault, whether amounting to careless/inconsiderate driving or not, and which contributes in some more than minimal way to the death" (at [36]).

The Supreme Court in *Taylor* declined to reverse the case of *Hughes*, and could not distinguish it. It found that the words "by driving a motor vehicle on a road" (in s.3ZB of the 1988 Act) and the words "owing to the driving of the vehicle, an accident occurred" (in s.12A of the 1968 Act) both "posit a direct connection between the driving and the injury" (at [22]).

Lord Sumption, delivering a unanimous judgement, referred to the presumption, articulated in *Sweet v Parsley* [1970] AC 132, that mens rea is an essential element of every offence. There were circumstances in which the law might impose strict liability. However, an aggravated vehicle-taking offence is punishable with two (or, where a death occurred, fourteen) years imprisonment, compared to six months for the basic offence. Attaching strict liability to the aggravating factor would mean that a "defendant is liable to be convicted and sentenced to a long period of imprisonment on account of an aggravating factor for which he bears no responsibility" (at [22]).

Theft, Taking Conveyances, Aggravated Vehicle-taking

The court ruled that a similar test to that in Hughes should be applied when determining causation in an offence under s.12A of the 1988 Act. To convict, a court must be satisfied that there was at least some act or omission in the control of the car, which involved some element of fault, whether amounting to careless/inconsiderate driving or not, which contributed in some more than minimal way to the accident.

The Supreme Court acknowledged that under s.12A, parties to the basic offence may be strictly liable for aggravated offences. Passengers who cannot establish a defence under s.12A(3) (either that the aggravating factor occurred before the basic offence, or that they were not in the immediate vicinity when that factor occurred) are guilty of the aggravated offence even when the Crown has not established mens rea for the aggravating factor. In this respect, the language of the Act unambiguously makes parties to a basic offence strictly liable. There is a legitimate justification for Parliament to depart from the presumption against strict liability, as parties to the basic offence are in a position to take positive steps to ensure that the taken vehicle is driven safely. Lord Sumption said:

> "However, it is one thing for the legislature to make a person who has taken a car without authority responsible for the fault of another person who drives it in his presence. It is another thing altogether to make him responsible for personal injury or damage which could not have been prevented, because it occurred without fault or was entirely the fault of the victim. That would be a sufficiently remarkable extension of the scope of the strict liability to require clear language, such as the draftsman has actually employed to impose liability on a taker who is not the driver. There is no such language in section 12A." (at [29].)

The court did not expand on how the provision will apply to parties to the basic offence. Presumably, if the prosecution cannot prove that the taker was at fault, the passenger should not be punished more severely either. Nor did the court address the issue as to proving the identity of the person at fault. One reason for introducing s.12A was that, in the words of the then Home Secretary:

> "[t]he Bill does not want any legal argument about the precise state of mind of those involved. It does not want to know whose foot was on the pedal, whose hand on the wheel or handbrake, or who might have said what to whom. The Bill is looking at the total aggravating consequences of the whole joyriding event, and it states that everyone guilty of taking, or travelling in the car should be liable for more serious punishment." (*Hansard*, December 9, 1991, vol 200, cols 620–686.)

It is also not clear from the judgement in *Taylor* whether all parties are to be found guilty even if the Crown can prove that any one of the parties to the taking was at fault. The court's acknowledgement that parties to the basic offence are strictly liable would suggest that they would be.

The concerns the Supreme Court identified in *Taylor*—that vehicle-takers might be liable for aggravating circumstances beyond their control—were considered during the passage of the Bill which became Aggravated Vehicle-Taking Act 1992. The Home Secretary explained to the House of Commons that one reason for that legislation was the difficulty in proving that the taker of a vehicle was responsible for accidents or damage that resulted after it had been taken. He emphasised that the Crown would still have to establish intent to commit the basic offence, but that those party to the basic offence should bear the consequences of that offence:

> "The Bill will not convict anybody of the crime of criminal damage, or the crime of reckless or dangerous driving, or any crime against the person. It is simply recognising an aggravated form of an existing Theft Act 1968 offence, where a vehicle is taken without the owner's consent, and damage, danger or injury follow which would not have happened if the vehicle had not been taken in the first place." (*Hansard*, December 9, 1991, vol 200, cols 620–686.)

In the House of Lords, Lord Airedale proposed an amendment to make it explicit that fault must be proved for an aggravated offence, by suggesting that s.12A(2)(b) and (c) should include the words "owing to the driving of the vehicle recklessly or carelessly, an accident occurred". In support, Lord Morris stated:

> "we have attempted to point out that the phrase: 'owing to the driving of the vehicle' must mean either owing to the fact that the vehicle was being driven or owing to the fact that the vehicle was being driven dangerously, recklessly, carelessly, badly or in some other way".

Earl Ferrers, speaking for the Government, opposed the amendment—not because he accepted Lord Morris' interpretation, but because the Bill was not intended to require fault:

> "The reason that the words 'owing to the driving of the vehicle' are important is because if [the taker of the vehicle] had not stolen and driven the car in the first place, the accident would never have occurred." (*Hansard*, March 3, 1992, vol 536, cols 812–832.)

In most cases where a death occurs, proof of causation for the accident will also establish causation for the death. However, there may be circumstances in which the Crown will have to establish causation for the death as well, if the higher penalty is to be invoked. Prosecutors must include the fact of the death in the indictment where they want the court to convict the accused of the more serious offence of aggravated vehicle-taking resulting in death (see § 15.36 of the main work).

The court in *R. v Taylor* was not required to consider offences aggravated by the fact that "damage was caused to the vehicle" under s.12A(2)(d). However, it suggested that such aggravating circumstance will not operate "independent of fault" (at [29]). Whilst the wording of s.12A(2)(d) makes no reference to the nature of the driving of the vehicle, damage is an aggravating factor which will increase the penalty for the offence (except where the value of the damage caused is under £5,000 and the maximum prison sentence remain six months). The wording also appears to require some element of mens rea, since a vehicle might be damaged accidentally or damaged by someone other than the taker. It can be argued, as it was when the Bill was being debated, that a person who takes a vehicle should be responsible for damage that might occur unless he can prove the statutory defence (that the damage was caused before the offence or that the accused was not in the vicinity when the damage was caused). It is difficult to see what other purpose Parliament had in passing the legislation, or the need for that statutory defence if the law requires the Crown to prove mens rea. Nevertheless, it seems unlikely that the Supreme Court would conclude that such a policy objective rebuts the requirement for establishing mens rea in the light of its comment in *Taylor*. It remains a matter of conjecture as to what level of fault is must be established.

The Aggravated Vehicle-Taking Bill was enacted using the fast-track procedure through the House of Commons—at that time, there was concern over the prevalence of such offences. Some members of Parliament expressed concern that the Bill went through all its stages in one day and did not go to a Standing Committee for full consideration (although the Bill went through a normal passage in the House of Lords). The only surprise, perhaps, is that the issues revealed in the case of *Taylor* have taken so long to surface.

There are likely to have been many cases over the years where defendants have pleaded guilty to aggravated offences on advice given in accordance with *R. v Marsh*, or have been convicted by a court applying that case. Applicants who are contemplating appealing against such convictions should consider the comments of the Court of Appeal (Criminal Division) in *R. v McGuffog* [2015] EWCA Crim 1116; [2015] R.T.R. 34 (see the note in this supplement: Chapter 22–Appeals, below), which conclude that the court will not grant an extension of time to appeal based solely upon a change in the law unless there has been a substantial injustice. An accused wrongly convicted of the aggravated offence is likely to have been guilty of the basic offence but, as previously observed, the penalties can be significantly greater—a conviction for an aggravated offence results in obligatory disqualification and a driving licence endorsement.

Chapter 18—Custodial and Other Penalties

Introduction

18.01   *Generally.* In accordance with what has now become normal practice, the Criminal Procedure Rules 2015 (SI 2015/1490) (as amended) have replaced the Criminal Procedure Rules 2014 (SI 2014/1610). The 2015 Rules came into effect on October 5, 2015 and were amended by SI 2016/120 with effect from April 4, 2016: Criminal Procedure (Amendment) Rules 2016 and by SI 2016/705 with effect from October 3, 2016: Criminal Procedure (Amendment No.2) Rules 2016. The rules were accompanied by new Criminal Practice Directions 2015 [2015] EWCA 1567 (as amended with effect from April 4, 2016: [2016] EWCA Crim 97). Few of the changes that have been made affect the rules or the directions referred to in the main work. Accordingly, unless specifically mentioned in this supplement, the number and content of the rules described in the main work remain the same. A main change in the Amendment No.2 Rules is the removal of the word "written" in a number of places related to the provision of notices; this reflects the move towards greater use of electronic transmission of information.

18.02   *Criminal Courts Charge.* See the note to § 18.12, below in this supplement.

18.02   *Code of Practice for Victims of Crime.* A revised Code has been published and was brought into force with effect from November 16, 2015; in part, the amendments are designed to incorporate minimum standards on the rights, supports and protection of victims of crime contained in Directive 2012/29/EU. The revised code and information sheets can be found at *https://www.gov.uk/government/publications/the-code-of-practice-for-victims-of-crime* (Accessed April 12, 2016). The Victim Personal Statement now incorporates the Family Impact Statement by widening who is considered to be a 'victim' for the purpose of creating a statement. The Practice Directions have been published in a revised form in October 2015 and the current version can be accessed at *http://www.justice.gov.uk/courts/procedure-rules/criminal/rulesmenu-2015* (Accessed April 12, 2016).

18.03   *Reduction for guilty plea.* The Sentencing Council issued a consultation paper on February 11, 2016 proposing revisions to the Guideline – this consultation paper can be accessed at *http://www.sentencingcouncil.org.uk/news/item/reduction-in-sentence-for-a-guilty-plea-consultation-launched-on-sentencing-guideline/* (Accessed April 12, 2016).

18.05   *The Magistrates' Courts Sentencing Guidelines.* The Sentencing Council has issued these guidelines in a new format making them easily accessible (and easily

36

updated) online—they can be seen at *http://www.sentencingcouncil.org.uk/the-magistrates-court-sentencing-guidelines/* (Accessed April 12, 2016).

Fines

The assessment and imposition of fines. The amount to be levied as a surcharge **18.10–** on those convicted of criminal offences (commonly known as the victims' sur- **18.11** charge) has been increased for those convicted of offences committed on or after April 8, 2016 by the Criminal Justice Act 2003 (Surcharge) (Amendment) Order 2016 (SI 2016/389). Where a person is convicted of more than one offence, all must be committed on or after April 8, 2016 for the new rates to apply.

TABLE 1

Column 1	Column 2
An order under section 12(1)(b) of the Powers of Criminal Courts (Sentencing) Act 2000 (conditional discharge)	£15
A fine	£20
An order under section 1 of the Criminal Justice and Immigration Act 2008 (youth rehabilitation orders)	£20
An order under section 16(2) or 16(3) of the Powers of Criminal Courts (Sentencing) Act 2000 (referral orders)	£20
An order under section 177(1) of the Criminal Justice Act 2003 (community orders)	£20
An order under section 189(1) of the Criminal Justice Act 2003 (suspended sentences of imprisonment)	£30
A sentence specified in section 76 of the Powers of Criminal Courts (Sentencing) Act 2000 (meaning of custodial sentence)	£30

TABLE 2

Column 1	Column 2
An order under section 12(1)(b) of the Powers of Criminal Courts (Sentencing) Act 2000 (conditional discharge)	£20
A fine	10 per cent of the value of the fine, rounded up or down to the nearest pound, which must be no less than £30 and no more than £170.
An order under section 177(1) of the Criminal Justice Act 2003 (community orders)	£85
An order under section 189(1) of the Criminal Justice Act 2003 (suspended sentences of imprisonment) where the sentence of imprisonment or detention in a young offender institution is for a period of 6 months or less	£115
An order under section 189(1) of the Criminal Justice Act 2003 (suspended sentences of imprisonment) where the sentence of imprisonment or detention in a young offender institution is for a determinate period of more than 6 months	£140
A sentence of imprisonment or detention in a young offender institution for a determinate period of up to and including 6 months	£115
A sentence of imprisonment or detention in a young offender institution for a determinate period of more than 6 months and up to and including 24 months	£140
A sentence of imprisonment or detention in a young offender institution for a determinate period exceeding 24 months	£170
A sentence of imprisonment or custody for life	£170

Custodial and Other Penalties

TABLE 3

Column 1	Column 2
An order under section 12(1)(b) of the Powers of Criminal Courts (Sentencing) Act 2000 (conditional discharge)	£20
A fine	10 per cent of the value of the fine, rounded up or down to the nearest pound, which must be no less than £30 and no more than £170.

Criminal Courts charge. To the great relief of many, the obligation to order pay- **18.12** ment of this charge has, in effect, been removed. Whilst the provisions inserted into the Prosecution of Offences Act 1985 remain in force, the relevant part of the Prosecution of Offences Act 1985 (Criminal Courts Charge) Regulations 2015 (SI 2015/796) has been repealed by the like named Amendment Regulations (SI 2015/1970), removing the specified amounts with effect from December 24, 2015.

Costs

The relevant part of the Criminal Procedure Rules 2015 (SI 2015/1490) is **18.45** r.29(3). This provides for endorsement of the 'sentence' but, it is submitted, the costs ordered are not part of the sentence.

Chapter 19—Endorsement and Penalty Points

Endorsement

19.01 *Generally.* In accordance with what has now become normal practice, the Criminal Procedure Rules 2015 (SI 2015/1490) (as amended) have replaced the Criminal Procedure Rules 2014 (SI 2014/1610). The 2015 Rules came into effect on October 5, 2015 and were amended by SI 2016/120 with effect from April 4, 2016: Criminal Procedure (Amendment) Rules 2016 and by SI 2016/705 with effect from October 3, 2016: Criminal Procedure (Amendment No.2) Rules 2016. The rules were accompanied by new Criminal Practice Directions 2015 [2015] EWCA 1567 (as amended with effect from April 4, 2016: [2016] EWCA Crim 97). Few of the changes that have been made affect the rules or the directions referred to in the main work. Accordingly, unless specifically mentioned in this supplement, the number and content of the rules described in the main work remain the same. A main change in the Amendment No.2 Rules is the removal of the word "written" in a number of places related to the provision of notices; this reflects the move towards greater use of electronic transmission of information.

19.05 *Requirement to endorse.* Rule 29.3 of the Criminal Procedure Rules 2015 now governs the requirements to endorse an offender's driving record. The requirements remain the same as those mentioned in the main work (previously r.55.2 of the 2014 Rules).

19.08 *Notification of endorsement.* Rule 29.3 of the Criminal Procedure Rules 2015 now governs the requirements of the court to notify the DVLA of the endorsement of an offender's driving record. The requirements remain the same as those mentioned in the main work (previously r.55.2 of the 2014 Rules).

Penalty Points

19.35 *Offences committed on the same occasion.* The High Court of Justiciary considered the case law relating to the endorsement of penalty points for offences committed "on the same occasion". The main work notes that courts have taken different views as to the meaning of the phrase. The High Court ruled in *Johnson v Finbow* [1983] 1 W.L.R. 879 that one offence committed after another may be regarded as being committed on the same occasion if they are linked in some way. Courts in Scotland have taken a more restrictive approach, concluding that "on the same occasion" did not mean "arising out of a single course of driving" (see *McKeever v Walkingshaw* (1995) 1996 S.T.L. 1228, which was followed in *Cameron v Brown* (1996) 1997 S.T.L. 914).

Endorsement and Penalty Points

In *MacLean v Procurator Fiscal, Stornoway* [2015] HCJAC 77, the appellant had pleaded guilty to careless driving and failing to report an accident. The sheriff had purported to order four points on each offence. The appellant conceded that, as the latter offence carried between five and ten points, the sheriff erred in imposing fewer than five points in respect of that offence. However, he contended only one set of points should have been ordered. The sheriff found that the two offences were not committed on the same occasion. He was of the view that the driving offence was committed on one day and the failure to report occurred sometime during the succeeding 24-hour period. He purported to follow the approach set out in the case of *Cameron v Brown*. Lord Matthews's judgment followed that case, in which Lord Cameron used the phrase "arising out of precisely the same incident", but noted that "[t]he obligation under section 170(3) to report to the police as soon as reasonably practicable and in any case within 24 hours of the accident arises immediately..." and concluded both offences were, therefore, committed on the same occasion.

Procedure on Conviction

Production of Driving Licence. The rules relating to service of documents have **19.39** changed. Rule 4.11 of the Criminal Procedure Rules 2015 now deals with deemed service for documents served by post, and r.4.12 allows service to be proved by certificate. The 2015 rules make no substantive changes.

Chapter 20—Disqualification

General Principles

20.01   *Generally.* In accordance with what has now become normal practice, the Criminal Procedure Rules 2015 (SI 2015/1490) (as amended) have replaced the Criminal Procedure Rules 2014 (SI 2014/1610). The 2015 Rules came into effect on October 5, 2015 and were amended by SI 2016/120 with effect from April 4, 2016: Criminal Procedure (Amendment) Rules 2016 and by SI 2016/705 with effect from October 3, 2016: Criminal Procedure (Amendment No.2) Rules 2016. The rules were accompanied by new Criminal Practice Directions 2015 [2015] EWCA 1567 (as amended with effect from April 4, 2016: [2016] EWCA Crim 97). Few of the changes that have been made affect the rules or the directions referred to in the main work. Accordingly, unless specifically mentioned in this supplement, the number and content of the rules described in the main work remain the same. A main change in the Amendment No.2 Rules is the removal of the word "written" in a number of places related to the provision of notices; this reflects the move towards greater use of electronic transmission of information.

20.20   *Period and commencement of disqualification.* The Court of Appeal has given guidance to courts on applying ss.35A and 35B of the Road Traffic Offenders Act 1988 in the case of *R. v Needham and others* [2016] EWCA Crim 455. The court determined that s.35A applies only to that part of a custodial sentence for which the disqualification is imposed; however, where a court also imprisons an offender for an unrelated offence the court should apply s.35B.

As the main work explains, s.35A requires a court to increase a disqualification imposed for an endorsable offence by half of any custodial sentence (the "extension period") it imposes for that offence. This is to ensure the offender serves the period that the court would otherwise have imposed on release. A similar provision covers disqualifications imposed for non-endorsable offences (s.147A of the Road Traffic Offender's Act 1988). The court is not required to impose such an "extension period" where it disqualifies an offender who is sent to custody for unrelated offences or is already serving such a sentence, but s.35B (and s.147B for non-endorsable offences) requires the court to have regard to the diminished effect of a disqualification as a punishment if the offender is in custody during all or part of the disqualification.

The provisions were inserted by s.137 of and Sch.16 to the Coroners and Justice Act 2009 which were themselves amended by s.30 of the Criminal Justice and Courts Act 2015 before they were brought into force.

Commencement

20.20a   The court in *Needham* noted that Schedule 22 of the 2009 Act was not signposted by any section of that Act. Whilst the court noted this was unusual it ruled that a signposting section was not essential to bringing into force the parts of Schedule 22 mentioned in the commencement order (Coroners and Justice Act 2009 (Commencement No.17) Order 2015 (SI 2015/819)) (at [10]).

By virtue of para.29 of Schedule 22 of the 2009 Act the provisions do not apply to offences committed wholly or partly before April 13, 2015. An offence is committed partly before that date if a "relevant event" occurred before that date. A "relevant event" is any act or event (including any consequence of an act) proof of which is required for conviction of the offence. The main work suggests that a literal reading of these provisions would appear to mean that a person who drives whilst disqualified after the commencement date but who was disqualified before that date would escape the consequences of the new provisions as the disqualification is a "relevant event" (being one the prosecutor has to prove). Treacy LJ (at [14]) disagreed with this conclusion saying that the prosecution need only prove that the accused was disqualified to prove the offence was committed. An accused disqualified before the commencement remained disqualified after that date; it seems, therefore, the Court of Appeal is of the view that it is unnecessary for the prosecution to prove the "event" of the disqualification to achieve a conviction, it merely needs to prove the fact that the accused was disqualified on the date of the alleged offence.

Applying the provisions

The Court of Appeal suggested courts should follow a four-step approach when applying the new legislation—a flow chart showing these steps is produced below. **20.20b**

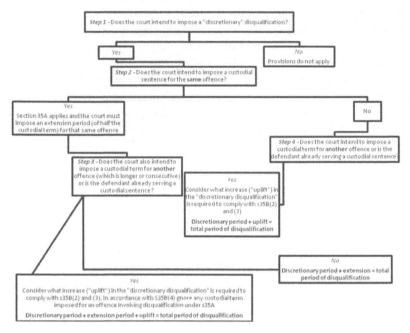

Treacy LJ noted that the legislation referred to the period that the court would have imposed were it not for the new legislation as the "discretionary period". Although the "discretionary period" was defined in the legislation, he observed that the term is a misnomer as it is defined to include a period of obligatory, as well as discretionary, disqualification.

He suggested that the principles articulated in *R. v Backhouse* [2010] EWCA Crim 1111 at [21] remained relevant. In that case, Treacy J (as he then was) said:

> "An order of disqualification has the purpose of protecting the public … disqualification is also intended to punish and deter offenders and others. A balance, however, has to be struck and the court should not disqualify for a period that is longer than necessary and should bear in mind the effects of a ban on employment or employment prospects."

This guidance holds good for judges calculating the "discretionary" element. The legislation then requires the court to add an "extension period" equating to half the custodial sentence when disqualifying an offender who is sent to custody. The purpose of the legislation is to ensure that generally a period of disqualification of an offender sent to custody should bite once released.

The court considered the position of an offender sent to custody for more than one offence, one of which is unrelated to the disqualification. It gave an example of an offender sentenced to one year for dangerous driving and nine years consecutively for an offence of violence. It concluded that the "extension period" required by s.35A related only to the custodial sentence for which the disqualification period was imposed and not the global custodial term (as the Crown had argued on appeal): this means that the "extension period" is six months rather five years. However, the effect of s.35B requires the court to have regard to the diminished effect of a disqualification where it sends an offender to custody for another offence. It should, therefore, apply an "uplift" to the disqualification to achieve a similar effect to that which is achieved by imposing an "extension period" under s.35A. However, Treacy LJ noted that courts have greater discretion when ordering an "uplift" under that provision than they do when ordering an "extension period" as they need have regard to the diminished effect of the disqualification only "if and to the extent that is appropriate". He conjectured that:

> "[i]n a case where a very lengthy custodial sentence is to be served for 'another offence' which is not motoring related, it might be anomalous or run counter to considerations of rehabilitation to impose a very long period of disqualification under section 35B in order that a comparatively short period of disqualification should take place after release from custody" (at [29]).

Originally the legislation had been drafted to require courts, when calculating an extended period, to reduce it to reflect the fact the accused would be released early because of time served on remand or on a bail curfew. The legislation was then amended to remove this exception. Consequently, a period of disqualification imposed on a defendant who is sentenced to custody but released immediately because he has served his sentence on remand must nevertheless be increased by an "extension period" where s.35A applies. The court could take account of the time served when calculating the "discretionary period" but where the court imposes the minimum period of disqualification permitted by the law it cannot reduce this. The court went on to say that a judge is not required to "fine tune the period of disqualification in order to accord with the precise calculation of release dates and periods spent on licence" (at [37]) nor does the court "envisage a precise arithmetical calculation taking place" (at [38]).

Interim disqualification

The court also pointed out that disqualifications starting when an offender is remanded in custody further complicates a judge's task when sentencing and suggested that interim disqualifications should not be imposed where offenders are remanded in custody. **20.20c**

Courses for drink drivers

The court also noted that legislation not yet brought into force will provide that reductions in disqualifications for offenders convicted of drink drive offences on successful completion of special courses (provided for by s.34A of the Road Traffic Offenders Act 1988) would be disregarded when calculating "extension periods". As this part of the legislation was not in force offenders will benefit. **20.20d**

"As presently in force any reduction in the disqualification period for attendance on courses would come off the entire disqualification including the extension period under section 35A." [44]

The legislation the court was referring to is Schedule 21, para.90(3) of the 2009 Act which will insert the words "disregarding any extension period added pursuant to section 35A or 35C" into subs.34A(3A) so it will read:

"'The reduced period' is the period of disqualification imposed under section 34 of this Act (disregarding any extension period added pursuant to section 35A or 35C) as reduced by an order under this section."

It should be noted that the reference to the provisions on the Sentencing Council website is misleading as it reads: "Where a rehabilitation course is completed, any extension period is disregarded when reducing the ban." (*http://www.sentencingcouncil.org.uk*: Magistrates' Court Sentencing Guidelines explanatory materials.) It is unclear when the Government intends to implement Schedule 21, para.90(3) of the 2009 Act.

Effect on Sentencing Guidelines

20.20e Treacy LJ considered the Sentencing Guidelines Council's guideline on causing death by dangerous driving which provides that the minimum disqualification should equate either to the period of imprisonment imposed (in the knowledge the offender will serve half) or the relevant statutory minimum, whichever is longer (at [31] of the guidelines) concluding that the courts should now focus on the legislation rather than the guidelines and not tailor the "discretionary period" to offenders' release dates but do so taking account of relevant factors including the need for public protection (at [46]).

Sentencing remarks

20.20f It is important that there is clarity when a sentence is announced and courts should announce the "discretionary period" and the "extension period" or, when disqualifying in cases where s.35B applies, indicate what part of any disqualification is accounted for by the "uplift" (at [48]).

Discretionary Disqualifications

20.54 *Disqualification where vehicle used for crime.* It is not wrong in principle to disqualify a driver convicted of exposing himself: *R. v Ketteridge* [2014] EWCA Crim 1962 [2015] 1 Cr. App. R. (S.) 11. The Court of Appeal upheld a disqualification where the offender was masturbating as he drove on a motorway. The judge had purported to disqualify him under both s.146 (the general power to disqualify) and s.147 (disqualification where vehicle used for purposes of crime) of the Powers of Criminal Courts (Sentencing) Act 2000, having concluded not only that the offences were indecent, but also that they created an obvious danger to other road users, because his attention was not on the road but on the young people at whom he was staring while controlling the vehicle with one hand on the steering wheel.

The Court of Appeal noted that a disqualification under s.146 applied to the commission of any offence and was intended to add to the court's powers of punishment of the offender. The power to disqualify under s.147 arose where the offence was punishable in the Crown Court with a sentence of two years or more, and where the court was satisfied that a motor vehicle was used for the purpose of committing or facilitating the commission of the offence. The appellant argued that the judge was wrong to disqualify him on the basis that the offence created a danger when he had not been charged with a driving offence. The Court of Appeal found that, as the offences were facilitated by his driving of his motor car, the judge was entitled to disqualify him under s.147 on that ground alone. In any event, the judge was not bound to ignore the obvious danger to other road users, particularly those on the M1 motorway. The disqualification was not wrong in principle, and nor was 12 months an excessive period.

Disqualification pending passing a driving test. The Road Traffic Offenders Act **20.68** 1988 and Motor Vehicles (Driving Licences) (Amendment) Regulations 2015 (SI 2015/2004) amend existing legislation in relation to Community licence holders who have been disqualified from driving in Great Britain until they have passed an appropriate test. A Community licence holder may drive a motor vehicle subject to the same conditions as a provisional licence holder whilst disqualified pending taking a test. The regulations also add a Community licence to the list of acceptable documents to demonstrate eligibility to take a driving test.

Disqualification on committal for sentence. Rule 28.10 of the Criminal Proce- **20.75** dure Rules 2015 replaces r. 42.10 of the 2014 Rules but makes no substantive change to the provisions.

Removal of Disqualification

Procedure for removal. Rule 29.2 of the Criminal Procedure Rules 2015 now **20.96** deals with the procedure for removal of disqualifications. This rule replaces r.55.1 of the 2014 rules but makes no substantive changes to it.

Chapter 21—Special Reasons and Mitigating Circumstances

21.01   *Generally.* In accordance with what has now become normal practice, the Criminal Procedure Rules 2015 (SI 2015/1490) (as amended) have replaced the Criminal Procedure Rules 2014 (SI 2014/1610). The 2015 Rules came into effect on October 5, 2015 and were amended by SI 2016/120 with effect from April 4, 2016: Criminal Procedure (Amendment) Rules 2016 and by SI 2016/705 with effect from October 3, 2016: Criminal Procedure (Amendment No.2) Rules 2016. The rules were accompanied by new Criminal Practice Directions 2015 [2015] EWCA 1567 (as amended with effect from April 4, 2016: [2016] EWCA Crim 97). Few of the changes that have been made affect the rules or the directions referred to in the main work. Accordingly, unless specifically mentioned in this supplement, the number and content of the rules described in the main work remain the same. A main change in the Amendment No.2 Rules is the removal of the word "written" in a number of places related to the provision of notices; this reflects the move towards greater use of electronic transmission of information.

Examples of Special Reasons

21.51   *Dangerous and careless driving.* The Sheriff Appeal Court found that a sheriff had been wrong not to find special reasons where a police driver had not activated her siren when she crossed a red light at a junction. The appellant was responding to a distress call and was displaying flashing blue lights when she crossed a junction at 10mph. She had collided with another vehicle. She pleaded guilty to dangerous driving but argued she should not be disqualified. The appeal court found that the fact she was not an accredited emergency driver irrelevant and a factor the sheriff should not have taken into account. Although it had been unfortunate that appellant had not activated her siren, she had considered the safety of others by slowing at the junction. She should not have been disqualified. The appeal court ruled, however, that her licence should be endorsed and penalty points imposed. As a new driver she would have been subject to the mandatory retest provisions had the court have ordered six penalty points or more (the range is between 3 and 11 points); in those circumstances the court endorsed her driving record with five points: *Watt (Natasha) v Murphy* [2016] SAC (Crim) 16.

Mitigating Circumstances: Excluded Grounds

21.70   *Hardship other than exceptional hardship.* The Sheriff Appeal Court decided that, where a disqualification would result in the loss of employment not just for the appellant but for 10 members of the staff of a small and specialised company which depended upon the appellant's expertise for its survival, the Justice should have found the existence of exceptional hardship established: *Waine v PF* [2016] SAC (Crim) 19.

Mitigating Circumstances: Practice and Procedure

Onus of proof, etc. Where a Sheriff had found mitigating circumstances it was **21.76** not open to him go on to impose a discretionary disqualification *Hamand v Harvie* [2016] SAC (Crim) 15. The appellant pleaded guilty to using a vehicle without insurance and using a mobile phone whilst driving. He sought to persuade the court there were mitigating circumstances for not disqualifying him under the totting provisions on the grounds of exceptional hardship. The sheriff found that there would be exceptional hardship if he were disqualified but then heard that the previously imposed points were for an offence of using a vehicle without insurance committed only a week before the offence he was dealing with. He disqualified the appellant for six months using his discretionary powers. The appellant argued that, by agreeing to hear arguments concerning mitigating circumstances, the court must have already ruled out a discretionary disqualification. The appeal court agreed and set aside the disqualification ordering eight penalty points instead and imposing no totting disqualification. Courts of first instance need to carefully consider their powers to exercise their powers of discretionary disqualification before hearing submissions as to mitigating circumstances. Defendants may also have to take care. It is not uncommon for offenders who are liable to be disqualified because of the number of points on their licence to put forward mitigating circumstances and, in the alternative, urge the court to impose a discretionary disqualification for a period shorter than the minimum totting disqualification should the court does not find mitigating circumstances. If this judgment is followed, such tactic would fail as the court should not proceed to hear evidence of mitigating circumstances until it has ruled out a discretionary disqualification. If this case is followed outside Scotland particular care will be needed as Part 29.1 of the Criminal Procedure Rules requires a court, where it is considering a totting disqualification, to explain that it must disqualify unless there are mitigating circumstances and invite an offender to give evidence of the same. If it gives such an explanation before ruling out a discretionary disqualification it might tie its own hands.

It difficult not to have sympathy with the sheriff in *Hamand v Harvie* who was, presumably, unaware of the details of the previous offence until he had ruled on the hardship argument. Section 35 of the Road Traffic Offenders Act 1988 gives the court discretion. It allows (rather than requires) a court to decide not to disqualify an offender at all or to disqualify for a shorter period that the statutory minimum if it finds there are mitigating circumstances. If the sheriff had decided that he was not satisfied, having regard to all the circumstances, that there were grounds for mitigating the normal consequences of the conviction notwithstanding the fact that the offender would be caused exceptional circumstances and proceeded to impose a totting disqualification the appeal may not have succeeded.

It is submitted that appeal courts will only interfere with a decision of the judge at first instance in such cases where it can be shown that decision was clearly wrong (see § 21.71 of the main work).

Chapter 22—Appeals

Introduction

Rights of Appeal: Generally. In accordance with what has now become normal **22.01** practice, the Criminal Procedure Rules 2015 (SI 2015/1490) (as amended) have replaced the Criminal Procedure Rules 2014 (SI 2014/1610). The 2015 Rules came into effect on October 5, 2015 and were amended by SI 2016/120 with effect from April 4, 2016: Criminal Procedure (Amendment) Rules 2016 and by SI 2016/705 with effect from October 3, 2016: Criminal Procedure (Amendment No.2) Rules 2016. The rules were accompanied by new Criminal Practice Directions 2015 [2015] EWCA 1567 (as amended with effect from April 4, 2016: [2016] EWCA Crim 97). Few of thechanges that have been made affect the rules or the directions referred to in the main work. Accordingly, unless specifically mentioned in this supplement, the number and content of the rules described in the main work remain the same. A main change in the Amendment No.2 Rules is the removal of the word "written" in a number of places related to the provision of notices; this reflects the move towards greater use of electronic transmission of information.

The Court of Appeal (Criminal Division) will not grant an extension of time to appeal based solely upon a change in the law unless a substantial injustice has taken place. However, where there has been a failure to act with proper expedition, but that delay was not the fault of the applicant and there was a substantial injustice, the court may exceptionally grant an extension. In *R. v McGuffog* [2015] EWCA Crim 1116; [2015] R.T.R. 34, the applicant had pleaded guilty to driving a motor vehicle on a road while unlicensed and thereby causing the deceased's death, contrary to s.3ZB of the 1988 Act. Subsequently, the Supreme Court ruled that, to convict a defendant of such an offence, the prosecution must show that the defendant's driving was at fault and that this contributed in some more than minimal way to the death (*R. v Hughes* [2013] R.T.R 31, see § 5.103 of the main work). The applicant's solicitors wrote to him about the case, but the letter was sent to the wrong address. The applicant waived his right to privilege and said he had entered his plea on the basis of advice according to the case law at the time, which stated that the offence could be committed without fault in the manner of his driving. The Crown conceded he was unlikely to have been convicted of the offence had he been tried after *Hughes* had been decided. The applicant had been disqualified from driving for five years and the cost of insurance was prohibitive as a consequence of his conviction. His 11-year-old daughter was disabled and his wife was entitled to a car under the Motability scheme, but the applicant could not drive. The court noted authorities which concluded that where an applicant would probably have been charged with another offence in such circumstances, the court would be unlikely to grant the extension (*R. (Amer)* [2006] EWCA Crim .1974; [2007] 1 Cr. App. R. 10 and *R. v Cottrell* [2007] 1 W.L.R. 3262). However, since the applicant was not responsible for the delay in the present case, he had served his sentence and continued to suffer the remoter consequences of his conviction, the court granted the extension.

22.03 *Appeals generally.* Rule 24.18 of the Criminal Procedure Rules 2015 ("Setting aside a conviction or varying a costs etc. order") now applies where a magistrates' court considers setting aside a conviction or costs order under the Magistrates' Courts Act 1980, s.142. Rule 28.4 of the 2015 Rules ("Variation of Sentence") applies where the Crown Court or a magistrates' court considers varying sentence (other than a costs order in the magistrates' court, which is dealt with under r.28.4). These rules supersede the previous provision under r.42.4 of the 2014 Rules.

22.04 The rules governing the extension of time limits for applying to the Crown Court to state a case for the opinion of the High Court are now contained in Pt 35 of the Criminal Procedure Rules 2015, but do not substantively change the provisions that were contained in Pt 64 of the 2014 Rules.

22.06 The Practice Direction (Costs in Criminal Proceedings) 2015 [2015] EWCA Crim 1568 has replaced the 2013 Direction referred to in the main work; however, the new direction has not altered the principle governing the making of an order for costs from central funds.

22.11 *Suspension of disqualification pending appeal.* The reference in the main work to r.68.3 of the Criminal Procedure Rules 2014 (Form of appeal notice), for the purpose of determining when an appeal is pending, should now be read as referring to r.39.3 of the 2015 Rules.

22.12 The reference to rr.63.2(2) and 63.3(1) of the Criminal Procedure Rules 2014 (Notice appeal and Form of notice) in the main work should now be read as references to rr.34.2 and 34.3 of the 2015 Rules.

Crown Court

22.16 *Scope of right and procedure.* The reference to rr.63.1–63.10 of the Criminal Procedure Rules 2014 (Appeals to the Crown Court) in the main work should now be read as references to Pt 34 of the 2015 Rules (as amended).

22.19 The reference to rr.63.1–63.10 of the Criminal Procedure Rules 2014 (Duty of the magistrates' court officer) in the main work should now be read as references to r.34.4 of the 2015 Rules.

22.23 The reference to r.64.5 of the Criminal Procedure Rules 2014 (Court's power to vary requirements under this Part) in the main work governing the procedure for asking the court to extend the time limit for asking the Crown Court to state a case for the opinion of the High Court should now be read as references to r.35.2(2) of the 2015 Rules.

Abandonment of appeal. The reference to Pt 78 of the Criminal Procedure Rules **22.26** 2014 (Costs) in the main work should now be read as references to Pt 45 of the 2015 Rules (as amended).

Constitution of the Crown Court. The rules governing the constitution of the **22.28** Crown Court when dealing with appeals from a magistrates' court are now contained in Pt 34 of the Criminal Procedure Rules 2015, which have been amended by r.11 of the Criminal Procedure (Amendment) Rules 2016. The rules now explicitly provide that a judge sitting alone can give case management directions and, if applicable, allow an appeal against conviction if the respondent prosecutor does not wish to oppose it. Rule 34.7 has been amended to provide for parties to apply for rulings when preparing for an appeal hearing.

High Court

Cases Stated. The reference in the main work to rr.64.1–64.5 of the Criminal **22.29** Procedure Rules 2014 should now be read as a reference to Pt 35 of the 2015 Rules. The following specific references to the rules should be noted:
- for r.64.3 of the 2014 Rules (Preparation of case stated), substitute r.35.3 of the 2015 Rules;
- for r.63.3 of the 2014 Rules (Form of appeal notice), substitute r.35.2 of the 2015 Rules; and
- for r.64.2 of the 2014 Rules (Application to State a Case), substitute r.35.3 of the 2015 Rules.

The reference in the main work to r.64.3(5) of the Criminal Procedure Rules **22.31** 2014 should now be read as a reference to r.33.5(5) of the 2015 Rules.

Appendix 2 Endorsement and Sentence Codes

DVLA Endorsement Codes

2A.02   The following codes should be added to those shown in the table in the main work.

Code	Offence	Penalty points
	Disqualified driver	
BA40	Causing death by driving while disqualified	3–11
BA60	Causing serious injury by driving while disqualified	3–11
	Drink or drugs	
DR31	Driving or attempting to drive then refusing to give permission for analysis of a blood sample that was taken without consent due to incapacity	3–11
DR61	Refusing to give permission for analysis of a blood sample that was taken without consent due to incapacity in circumstances other than driving or attempting to drive	10
DG10	Driving or attempting to drive with a drug level above the specified limit	3–11
DG60	Causing death by careless driving with drug level above the limit	3–11
DG40	In charge of a vehicle while drug level above specified limit	10
DG80	Driving or attempting to drive when unfit through drugs	3–11

Appendix 3 Sentencing Guidelines

The Magistrates' Court Sentencing Guidelines were being reviewed and the **3A.01** closing date for consultation was August 12, 2016. The Guidelines are now available in electronic form at *http://www.sentencingcouncil.org.uk/the-magistrates-court-sentencing-guidelines* and will be updated as needed. They can be downloaded also as a PDF document from the same page. The Sentencing Council has also been reviewing the guidelines relating to the imposition of community and custodial sentences and these are due to be published in October 2016. As this is after the date to which this has worked, any relevant changes will be incorporated into the 28th Edition.

The main changes to the guidelines shown in the main work are: **3A.28**

- to note that fines should generally be payable within 12 months, although recognising that there will be exceptions to this (Approach to the assessment of fines, para.3; § 3A.28 of the main work);
- to add fine bands D–F (Approach to the assessment of fines, para.5; § 3A.28 of the main work);
- to note changes to deemed income levels (Approach to the assessment of fines, paras 7–14; § 3A.28 of the main work);
- to make references to the introduction of unlimited fines for certain offences (Approach to the assessment of fines, paras 25 and 29; § 3A.28 of the main work);
- to reflect changes to the surcharge which must be levied when a fine is imposed (Approach to the assessment of fines, paras 30–32; § 3A.28 of the main work);
- to take account of the guidance on costs given in *R. v Northallerton Magistrates' Court, ex p. Dove* [2000] 1 Cr. App. R. (S) 136, CA (Approach to the assessment of fines, para.33; § 3A.28 of the main work);
- changes to the guidance concerning disqualification in absence (Disqualification, para.23; § 3A.31 of the main work); and
- to reflect the changes made to take account of Criminal Justice and Courts Act 2015 which introduces requirements to extend disqualifications where an offender receives a custodial sentence (Disqualification, para.25; § 3A.31 of the main work).

Noter–up to Volume 1

Approach to the assessment of fines

Introduction

1. The amount of a fine must reflect the seriousness of the offence.[1]

2. The court must also take into account the financial circumstances of the offender; this applies whether it has the effect of increasing or reducing the fine.[2]

3. The aim is for the fine to have an equal impact on offenders with different financial circumstances; it should be a hardship but should not force the offender below a reasonable 'subsistence' level. Normally a fine should be of an amount that is capable of being paid within 12 months though there may be exceptions to this.

4. The guidance below aims to establish a clear, consistent and principled approach to the assessment of fines that will apply fairly in the majority of cases. However, it is impossible to anticipate every situation that may be encountered and in each case the court will need to exercise its judgment to ensure that the fine properly reflects the seriousness of the offence and takes into account the financial circumstances of the offender.

Fine bands

5. For the purpose of the offence guidelines, a fine is usually based on one of three bands (A, B or C). The selection of the relevant fine band, and the position of the individual offence within that band, is determined by the seriousness of the offence. In some cases fine bands D – F may be used even where the community or custody threshold have been passed.

	Starting point	Range
Fine Band A	50% of relevant weekly income	25 – 75% of relevant weekly income
Fine Band B	100% of relevant weekly income	75 – 125% of relevant weekly income
Fine Band C	150% of relevant weekly income	125 – 175% of relevant weekly income
Fine Band D	250% of relevant weekly income	200 – 300% of relevant weekly income
Fine Band E	400% of relevant weekly income	300 – 500% of relevant weekly income
Fine Band F	600% of relevant weekly income	500 – 700% of relevant weekly income

6. For an explanation of the meaning of starting point and range, both generally and in relation to fines, see pages 16-17.

Definition of relevant weekly income

7. The seriousness of an offence determines the choice of fine band and the position of the offence within the range for that band. The offender's financial circumstances are taken into account by expressing that position as a proportion of the offender's relevant weekly income.

8. Where:

- an offender is in receipt of income from employment or is self-employed **and**
- that income is **more than £120** per week after deduction of tax and national insurance (or equivalent where the offender is self-employed),
the actual income is the relevant weekly income.

---

[1] Criminal Justice Act 2003 s.164(2)
[2] Ibid ss. 164(3) and 164(4)

148

Sentencing Guidelines

9. Where:

- an offender's only source of income is state benefit (including where there is relatively low additional income as permitted by the benefit regulations) **or**
- the offender is in receipt of income from employment or is self-employed but the amount of income after deduction of tax and national insurance is **£120 per week or less**,

the **relevant weekly income is deemed to be £120**.

Additional information about the basis for this approach is set out in paragraphs 26-31 below.

10. In calculating relevant weekly income no account should be taken of tax credits, housing benefit, child benefit or similar.

No reliable information

11. Where an offender has failed to provide information, or the court is not satisfied that it has been given sufficient reliable information, it is entitled to make such determination as it thinks fit regarding the financial circumstances of the offender.[3] Any determination should be clearly stated on the court records for use in any subsequent variation or enforcement proceedings. In such cases, a record should also be made of the applicable fine band and the court's assessment of the position of the offence within that band based on the seriousness of the offence.

12. Where there is no information on which a determination can be made, the court should proceed on the basis of an assumed **relevant weekly income of £440**. This is derived from national median pre- tax earnings; a gross figure is used as, in the absence of financial information from the offender, it is not possible to calculate appropriate deductions.[4]

13. Where there is some information that tends to suggest a significantly lower or higher income than the recommended £440 default sum, the court should make a determination based on that information.

14. A court is empowered to remit a fine in whole or part if the offender subsequently provides information as to means.[5] The assessment of offence seriousness and, therefore, the appropriate fine band and the position of the offence within that band are not affected by the provision of this information.

Assessment of financial circumstances

15. While the initial consideration for the assessment of a fine is the offender's relevant weekly income, the court is required to take account of the offender's financial circumstances including assets more broadly. Guidance on important parts of this assessment is set out below.

16. An offender's financial circumstances may have the effect of increasing or reducing the amount of the fine; however, they are not relevant to the assessment of offence seriousness. They should be considered separately from the selection of the appropriate fine band and the court's assessment of the position of the offence within the range for that band.

Out of the ordinary expenses

17. In deciding the proportions of relevant weekly income that are the starting points and ranges for each fine band, account has been taken of reasonable living expenses. Accordingly, no further allowance should normally be made for these. In addition, no allowance should normally be made where the offender has dependants.

18. Outgoings will be relevant to the amount of the fine only where the expenditure is out of the ordinary and substantially reduces the ability to pay a financial penalty so that the requirement to

---

[3] Criminal Justice Act 2003, s.164(5)
[4] This figure is a projected estimate based upon the 2012-13 Survey of Personal Incomes using economic assumptions consistent with the Office for Budget Responsibility's March 2015 economic and fiscal outlook. The latest actual figure is for 2012-13, when median pre-tax income was £404 per week (https://www.gov.uk/government/statistics/shares-of-total-income-before-and-after-tax-and-income-tax-for-percentile-groups).
[5] Criminal Justice Act 2003, s.165(2)

149

pay a fine based on the standard approach would lead to undue hardship.

Unusually low outgoings

19. Where the offender's living expenses are substantially lower than would normally be expected, it may be appropriate to adjust the amount of the fine to reflect this. This may apply, for example, where an offender does not make any financial contribution towards his or her living costs.

Savings

20. Where an offender has savings these will not normally be relevant to the assessment of the amount of a fine although they may influence the decision on time to pay.

21. However, where an offender has little or no income but has substantial savings, the court may consider it appropriate to adjust the amount of the fine to reflect this.

Household has more than one source of income

22. Where the household of which the offender is a part has more than one source of income, the fine should normally be based on the income of the offender alone.

23. However, where the offender's part of the income is very small (or the offender is wholly dependent on the income of another), the court may have regard to the extent of the household's income and assets which will be available to meet any fine imposed on the offender.[6]

Potential earning capacity

24. Where there is reason to believe that an offender's potential earning capacity is greater than his or her current income, the court may wish to adjust the amount of the fine to reflect this.[7] This may apply, for example, where an unemployed offender states an expectation to gain paid employment within a short time. The basis for the calculation of fine should be recorded in order to ensure that there is a clear record for use in variation or enforcement proceedings.

High income offenders

25. Where the offender is in receipt of very high income, a fine based on a proportion of relevant weekly income may be disproportionately high when compared with the seriousness of the offence. In such cases, the court should adjust the fine to an appropriate level; as a general indication, in most cases the fine for a first time offender pleading not guilty should not exceed 75% of the maximum fine. In the case of fines which are unlimited the court should decide the appropriate level with the guidance of the legal adviser.

Approach to offenders on low income

26. An offender whose primary source of income is state benefit will generally receive a base level of benefit (e.g. jobseeker's allowance, a relevant disability benefit or income support) and may also be eligible for supplementary benefits depending on his or her individual circumstances (such as child tax credits, housing benefit, council tax benefit and similar). In some cases these benefits may have been replaced by Universal Credit.

27. If relevant weekly income were defined as the amount of benefit received, this would usually result in higher fines being imposed on offenders with a higher level of need; in most circumstances that would not properly balance the seriousness of the offence with the financial circumstances of the offender. While it might be possible to exclude from the calculation any allowance above the basic entitlement of a single person, that could be complicated and time consuming.

---

[6] *R v Engen* [2004] EWCA Crim 1536 (CA)
[7] *R v Little* (unreported) 14 April 1976 (CA)

Sentencing Guidelines

28. Similar issues can arise where an offender is in receipt of a low earned income since this may trigger eligibility for means related benefits such as working tax credits and housing benefit depending on the particular circumstances. It will not always be possible to determine with any confidence whether such a person's financial circumstances are significantly different from those of a person whose primary source of income is state benefit.

29. For these reasons, a simpler and fairer approach to cases involving offenders in receipt of low income (whether primarily earned or as a result of benefit) is to identify an amount that is deemed to represent the offender's relevant weekly income.

30. While a precise calculation is neither possible nor desirable, it is considered that an amount that is approximately half-way between the base rate for jobseeker's allowance and the net weekly income of an adult earning the minimum wage for 30 hours per week represents a starting point that is both realistic and appropriate; this is currently £120.[8] The calculation is based on a 30 hour working week in recognition of the fact that many of those on minimum wage do not work a full 37 hour week and that lower minimum wage rates apply to younger people.

31. The figures will be updated in due course in accordance with any changes to benefit and minimum wage levels.

Offence committed for 'commercial' purposes

32. Some offences are committed with the intention of gaining a significant commercial benefit. These often occur where, in order to carry out an activity lawfully, a person has to comply with certain processes which may be expensive. They include, for example, 'taxi-touting' (where unauthorised persons seek to operate as taxi drivers) and 'fly-tipping' (where the cost of lawful disposal is considerable).

33. In some of these cases, a fine based on the standard approach set out above may not reflect the level of financial gain achieved or sought through the offending. Accordingly:

   (a) where the offender has generated income or avoided expenditure to a level that can be calculated or estimated, the court may wish to consider that amount when determining the financial penalty;

   (b) where it is not possible to calculate or estimate that amount, the court may wish to draw on information from the enforcing authorities about the general costs of operating within the law.

Offence committed by an organisation

34. Where an offence is committed by an organisation, guidance on fines can be found at in the environmental offences guideline at page 308.

35. See the Criminal Practice Direction CPD XIII Listing Annex 3 for directions on dealing with cases involving very large fines in the magistrates' court.[9]

---

[8] With effect from 1 October 2014, the minimum wage is £6.50 per hour for an adult aged 21 or over. Based on a 30 hour week, this equates to approximately £189 after deductions for tax and national insurance. To ensure equivalence of approach, the level of jobseeker's allowance for a single person aged 18 to 24 has been used for the purpose of calculating the mid point; this is currently £57.90.
[9] https://www.justice.gov.uk/courts/procedure-rules/criminal/rulesmenu

Reduction for a guilty plea

36. Where a guilty plea has been entered, the amount of the fine should be reduced by the appropriate proportion. Courts should refer to the *Guilty Plea* guideline.

Maximum fines

37. A fine must not exceed the statutory limit. Where this is expressed in terms of a 'level', the maxima are:

Level 1	£200
Level 2	£500
Level 3	£1,000
Level 4	£2,500
Level 5	unlimited[10]

See the Criminal Practice Direction XIII Listing Annex 3 for directions on dealing with cases involving very large fines in the magistrates' court.[11]

Multiple offences

38. Where an offender is to be fined for two or more offences that arose out of the same incident, it will often be appropriate to impose on the most serious offence a fine which reflects the totality of the offending where this can be achieved within the maximum penalty for that offence. 'No separate penalty' should be imposed for the other offences.

39. Where compensation is being ordered, that will need to be attributed to the relevant offence as will any necessary ancillary orders.

Imposition of fines with custodial sentences

40. A fine and a custodial sentence may be imposed for the same offence although there will be few circumstances in which this is appropriate, particularly where the custodial sentence is to be served immediately. One example might be where an offender has profited financially from an offence but there is no obvious victim to whom compensation can be awarded. Combining these sentences is most likely to be appropriate only where the custodial sentence is short and/or the offender clearly has, or will have, the means to pay.

41. Care must be taken to ensure that the overall sentence is proportionate to the seriousness of the offence and that better off offenders are not able to 'buy themselves out of custody'.

42. Consult your legal adviser if considering lodging fines or costs on the imposition of a custodial sentence.

Consult your legal adviser in any case in which you are considering combining a fine with a custodial sentence.

---

[10] for offences committed after 13 March 2015. For offences committed before that date the level 5 maximum is £5,000
[11] https://www.justice.gov.uk/courts/procedure-rules/criminal/rulesmenu

152

Sentencing Guidelines

Payment

43. A fine is payable in full on the day on which it is imposed. The offender should always be asked for immediate payment when present in court and some payment on the day should be required wherever possible.

44. Where that is not possible, the court may, in certain circumstances,[12] require the offender to be detained. More commonly, a court will allow payments to be made over a period set by the court:

    (a)   if periodic payments are allowed, the fine should normally be payable within a maximum of 12 months.

    (b)   compensation should normally be payable within 12 months. However, in exceptional circumstances it may be appropriate to allow it to be paid over a period of up to 3 years.

45. Where fine bands D, E and F apply (see paragraph 5 above), it may be appropriate for the fine to be of an amount that is larger than can be repaid within 12 months. In such cases, the fine should normally be payable within a maximum of 18 months (band D) or 2 years (bands E and F).

46. When allowing payment by instalments **payments should be set at a realistic rate taking into account the offender's disposable income.** The following approach may be useful:

Net weekly income	**Suggested** starting point for weekly payment
£60	£5
£120	£10
£200	£25
£300	£50
£400	£80

If the offender has dependants or larger than usual commitments, the weekly payment is likely to be decreased.

47. The payment terms must be included in any collection order made in respect of the amount imposed; see below.

Collection orders

48. The Courts Act 2003 created a fines collection scheme which provides for greater administrative enforcement of fines. Consult your legal adviser for further guidance.

Attachment of earnings orders/applications for benefit deductions

49. Unless it would be impracticable or inappropriate to do so, the court must make an attachment of earnings or (AEO) or application for benefit deductions (ABD) whenever:

- compensation is imposed;[13] or
- the court concludes that the offender is an existing defaulter and that the existing default cannot be disregarded.[14]

50. In other cases, the court may make an AEO or ABD with the offender's consent.[15]

---

[12] See section 82 of the Magistrates' Court Act for restrictions on the power to impose imprisonment on default.
[13] Courts Act 2003, sch. 5, para. 7A
[14] ibid., para.8
[15] ibid., para.9

153

51. The court must make a collection order in every case in which a fine or compensation order is imposed unless this would be impracticable or inappropriate.[16] The collection order must state:

- the amount of the sum due, including the amount of any fine, compensation order or other sum;

- whether the court considers the offender to be an existing defaulter;

- whether an AEO or ABD has been made and information about the effect of the order;

- if the court has not made an AEO or ABD, the payment terms;

- if an AEO or ABD has been made, the reserve terms (i.e. the payment terms that will apply if the AEO or ABD fails). It will often be appropriate to set a reserve term of payment in full within 14 days.

---

[16] ibid., para.12
154

MCSG explanatory materials - updated August 2015

Road traffic offences - disqualification

Obligatory disqualification

1. Some offences carry obligatory disqualification for a minimum of 12 months.[54] The minimum period is automatically increased where there have been certain previous convictions and disqualifications.

2. An offender must be disqualified for at least two years if he or she has been disqualified two or more times for a period of at least 56 days in the three years preceding the commission of the offence.[55] The following disqualifications are to be disregarded for the purposes of this provision:

    *   interim disqualification;

    *   disqualification where vehicle used for the purpose of crime;

    *   disqualification for stealing or taking a vehicle or going equipped to steal or take a vehicle.

3. An offender must be disqualified for at least three years if he or she is convicted of one of the following offences <u>and</u> has within the ten years preceding the commission of the offence been convicted of any of these offences:[56]

    *   causing death by careless driving when under the influence of drink or drugs;

    *   driving or attempting to drive while unfit;

    *   driving or attempting to drive with excess alcohol;

    *   failing to provide a specimen (drive/attempting to drive).

4. The individual offence guidelines above indicate whether disqualification is mandatory for the offence and the applicable minimum period. **Consult your legal adviser for further guidance.**

Special Reasons

5. The period of disqualification may be reduced or avoided if there are special reasons.[57] These must relate to the offence; circumstances peculiar to the offender cannot constitute special reasons.[58] The Court of Appeal has established that, to constitute a special reason, a matter must:[59]

    *   be a mitigating or extenuating circumstance;

    *   not amount in law to a defence to the charge;

    *   be directly connected with the commission of the offence;

    *   be one which the court ought properly to take into consideration when imposing sentence.

Consult your legal adviser for further guidance on special reasons applications.

---

[54] Road Traffic Offenders Act 1988, s.34
[55] ibid., s.34(4)
[56] ibid., s.34(3)
[57] ibid., s.34(1)
[58] *Whittal v Kirby* [1946] 2 All ER 552 (CA)
[59] *R v Wickens* (1958) 42 Cr App R 436 (CA)

'Totting up' disqualification

6. Disqualification for a minimum of six months must be ordered if an offender incurs 12 penalty points or more within a three-year period.[60] The minimum period may be automatically increased if the offender has been disqualified within the preceding three years. Totting up disqualifications, unlike other disqualifications, erase all penalty points.

7. The period of a totting up disqualification may be reduced or avoided for exceptional hardship or other mitigating circumstances if the court thinks fit to do so. No account is to be taken of hardship that is not exceptional hardship or circumstances alleged to make the offence not serious. Any circumstances taken into account in the preceding three years to reduce or avoid a totting disqualification must be disregarded.[61]

8. **Consult your legal adviser for further guidance on exceptional hardship applications.**

Discretionary disqualification

9. Whenever an offender is convicted of an endorsable offence or of taking a vehicle without consent, the court has a discretionary power to disqualify instead of imposing penalty points. The individual offence guidelines above indicate whether the offence is endorsable and the number or range of penalty points it carries.

10. The number of variable points or the period of disqualification should reflect the seriousness of the offence. Some of the individual offence guidelines above include penalty points and/or periods of disqualification in the sentence starting points and ranges; however, the court is not precluded from sentencing outside the range where the facts justify it. Where a disqualification is for less than 56 days, there are some differences in effect compared with disqualification for a longer period; in particular, the licence will automatically come back into effect at the end of the disqualification period (instead of requiring application by the driver) and the disqualification is not taken into account for the purpose of increasing subsequent obligatory periods of disqualification.[62]

11. In some cases in which the court is considering discretionary disqualification, the offender may already have sufficient penalty points on his or her licence that he or she would be liable to a 'totting up' disqualification if further points were imposed. In these circumstances, the court should impose penalty points rather than discretionary disqualification so that the minimum totting up disqualification period applies (see paragraph 6 above).

Disqualification until a test is passed

12. Where an offender is convicted of dangerous driving, the court must order disqualification until an extended driving test is passed.

13. The court has discretion to disqualify until a test is passed where an offender is convicted of any endorsable offence.[63] Where disqualification is obligatory, the extended test applies. In other cases, it will be the ordinary test.

14. An offender disqualified as a 'totter' under the penalty points provisions may also be ordered to re-take a driving test; in this case, the extended test applies.

15. The discretion to order a re-test is likely to be exercised where there is evidence of inexperience, incompetence or infirmity, or the disqualification period is lengthy (that is, the offender is going to be 'off the road' for a considerable time).

---

[60] Road Traffic Offenders Act 1988, s.35
[61] ibid.
[62] ibid. ss34(4), 35(2), 37(1A)
[63] ibid. s36(4)
182

Sentencing Guidelines

MCSG explanatory materials - updated August 2015

Reduced period of disqualification for completion of rehabilitation course

16. Where an offender is disqualified for 12 months or more in respect of an alcohol-related driving offence, the court may order that the period of disqualification will be reduced if the offender satisfactorily completes an approved rehabilitation course.[64]

17. Before offering an offender the opportunity to attend a course, the court must be satisfied that an approved course is available and must inform the offender of the effect of the order, the fees that the offender is required to pay, and when he or she must pay them.

18. The court should also explain that the offender may be required to satisfy the Secretary of State that he or she does not have a drink problem and is fit to drive before the offender's licence will be returned at the end of the disqualification period.[65]

19. In general, a court should consider offering the opportunity to attend a course to all offenders convicted of a relevant offence for the first time. The court should be willing to consider offering an offender the opportunity to attend a second course where it considers there are good reasons. It will not usually be appropriate to give an offender the opportunity to attend a third course.

20. The reduction must be at least three months but cannot be more than one quarter of the total period of disqualification:

    - a period of 12 months disqualification must be reduced to nine months;

    - in other cases, a reduction of one week should be made for every month of the disqualification so that, for example, a disqualification of 24 months will be reduced by 24 weeks.

21. When it makes the order, the court must specify a date for completion of the course which is at least two months before the end of the reduced period of disqualification.

Disqualification in the offender's absence

22. When considering disqualification in absence the starting point should be that disqualification in absence should be imposed if there is no reason to believe the defendant is not aware of the proceedings, and after the statutory notice has been served pursuant to section 11(4) of the Magistrates' Courts Act 1980 where appropriate. Disqualification should not be imposed in absence where there is evidence that the defendant has an acceptable reason for not attending or where there are reasons to believe it would be contrary to the interests of justice to do so.

New drivers

23. Drivers who incur six points or more during the two-year probationary period after passing the driving test will have their licence revoked automatically by the Secretary of State; they will be able to drive only after application for a provisional licence pending the passing of a further test.[66]

24. An offender liable for an endorsement which will cause the licence to be revoked under the new drivers' provisions may ask the court to disqualify rather than impose points. This will avoid the requirement to take a further test. Generally, this would be inappropriate since it would circumvent the clear intention of Parliament.

---

[64] Road Traffic Offenders Act 1988 s.34A
[65] Road Traffic Act 1988
[66] Road Traffic (New Drivers) Act 1995

Extension period of disqualification from driving where a custodial sentence is also imposed

25.   Where a court imposes disqualification in addition to a custodial sentence or a detention and training order, the court must extend the disqualification period by one half of the custodial sentence or detention or training order to take into account the period the offender will spend in custody. This will avoid a driving ban expiring, or being significantly diminished, during the period the offender is in custody (s.35a Criminal Justice and Courts Act, 2015). Periods of time spent on remand or subject to an electronically monitored curfew do not apply.

26.   Where a rehabilitation course is completed, any extension period is disregarded when reducing the ban.

27.   For example where a court imposes a 6 month custodial sentence and a disqualification period of 12 months, the ban will be extended to 15 months. Where a rehabilitation course is completed, the reduction will remain at a maximum of 3 months.

183a

Noter-up to Volume 2

Contents

Noter-up to Volume 2

Legislation

Section A: Statutes

Transport Act 1968 (1968 c.73)

Section 96A. With effect from March 2, 2016, the following paragraph has been inserted after section 96 by the Passenger and Goods Vehicles (Tachographs) (Amendment) Regulations 2016 (SI 2016/248):

A4.06a

[Authorisation of field tests

96A.—(1) The Secretary of State may authorise a person to carry out tests ("field tests") of—

(a) recording equipment that has not been type-approved under Article 13 of the EU Tachographs Regulation (granting of type-approval), or

(b) modifications or additions to recording equipment that has been so approved.

(2) An authorisation is to be in writing.

(3) The Secretary of State may withdraw an authorisation by giving written notice.

(4) An authorisation may contain conditions which may in particular relate to—

(a) the places where and equipment by means of which a field test is, or is to be, carried out;

(b) the procedure to be adopted in carrying out a field test;

(c) the records to be kept and the evidence to be furnished of the carrying out of a field test;

(d) the training of persons for carrying out field tests;

(e) the inspection by or on behalf of the Secretary of State of places where and equipment by means of which field tests are, or are to be, carried out;

(f) the display, at the places where field tests are carried out, of signs indicating that field tests are carried out there by persons approved by the Secretary of State.

(5) The Secretary of State must from time to time publish lists of the persons currently authorised under this section.]

Section 97. With effect from March 2, 2016, the following amendments have been made to section 97 by the Passenger and Goods Vehicles (Tachographs) (Amendment) Regulations 2016 (SI 2016/248):

A4.07

1. In sub-para.(1)—

(a) in paragraph (a)(i), the words "EU Tachographs Regulation" have been substituted for the words "Community Recording Equipment Regulation";

(b) in paragraph (a)(iii), the words "27 to 29 and 32 to 37" have been substituted for the words "13 to 15";

(c) in paragraph (b), the words "EU Tachographs Regulation" have been substituted for the words "Community Recording Equipment Regulation".

2. In sub-paras (1A) and (2) the words "EU Tachographs Regulation" have been substituted for the words "Community Recording Equipment Regulation".

3. In sub-para.(3)(b) the words "Article 37(2) of the EU Tachographs Regulation" have been substituted for the words "Article 16(2) of the Community Recording Equipment Regulation".

4. In sub-para.(4)(c) the words "Articles 27 to 29 and 32 to 37 of the EU Tachographs Regulation" have been substituted for the words "Article 13 to 15 of the Community Recording Equipment Regulation".

5. In sub-para.(4A)—

(a) in paragraph (b), the words "Articles 29(2) to (5), 35 and 37(2)" of the EU Tachographs Regulation" have been substituted for the words "Article 16(2) and, apart from the last paragraph thereof, Article 16(3) of the Community Recording Equipment Regulation";

(b) in paragraph (c), the words "Articles 27 to 29 and 32 to 37" have been substituted for the words "Articles 13 to 15".

6. After sub-para.(4A), the following sub-paras have been inserted—

[(4B) A person shall not be liable to be convicted under subsection (1) of this section by reason of using recording equipment which does not bear a type-approval mark issued under Article 14 of the EU Tachographs Regulation if he proves to the court that the use of the recording equipment was in the course of a field test authorised under section 96A.

(4C) Where a person ("the driver")—

(a) in the course of the driver's employment, uses a vehicle in contravention of subsection (1), and

(b) is liable to be convicted under that subsection in respect of that use, the employer also commits an offence and shall be liable on summary conviction to a fine.

(4D) A person shall not be liable to be convicted under subsection (4C) in respect of the use of a vehicle if the requirements of Article 10(1) and (2) of the Community Drivers' Hours Regulation (liability of transport undertakings) and Article 33(1) of the EU Tachographs Regulation (responsibility of transport undertakings) were complied with in relation to that use.]

7. In sub-para.(5), the words "Articles 27 to 29 and 32 to 37 of the EU Tachographs Regulation" have been substituted for the words "Article 13 to 15 of the Community Recording Equipment Regulation".

8. In sub-para.(6), the words "EU Tachographs Regulation" have been substituted for the words "Community Recording Equipment Regulation".

9. In sub-para.(7), the definition of "the Community Recording Equipment Regulation" has been substituted as follows—

["*the EU Tachographs Regulation*" means Regulation (EU) No. 165/2014 of the European Parliament and of the Council on tachographs in road transport as read with the Community Drivers' Hours and Recording Equipment Regulations 2007 (S.I. 2007/1819);]

Section 97B. With effect from March 2, 2016, section 97B(2) has been amended **A4.12** by the Passenger and Goods Vehicles (Tachographs) (Amendment) Regulations 2016 (SI 2016/248) such that the words "Article 34(1), (3), (4) or (6) or 37(2) of the EU Tachographs Regulation" have been substituted for the words "Article 15(2) or (5) or 16(2) of the Community Recording Equipment Regulation".

Section 97C. With effect from March 2, 2016, section 97C(1)(b) has been **A4.14** amended by the Passenger and Goods Vehicles (Tachographs) (Amendment) Regulations 2016 (SI 2016/248) such that the words "EU Tachographs Regulation" have been substituted for the words "Community Recording Equipment Regulation".

Section 97D. With effect from March 2, 2016, section 97D(8) has been amended **A4.16** by the Passenger and Goods Vehicles (Tachographs) (Amendment) Regulations 2016 (SI 2016/248) such that the words "Article 2(2)(n) of the EU Tachographs Regulation" have been substituted for the words "Annex 1B to the Community Recording Equipment Regulation".

Section 99ZA. With effect from March 2, 2016, the following amendments have **A4.30** been made to section 99ZA by the Passenger and Goods Vehicles (Tachographs) (Amendment) Regulations 2016 (SI 2016/248):

1. in sub-para.(1)(b) the words "EU Tachographs Regulation" have been substituted for the words "Community Recording Equipment Regulation";
2. in sub-para.(2)(a) the words "Article 36 of the EU Tachographs Regulation" have been substituted for the words "Article 15(7) of the Community Recording Equipment Regulation";
3. in sub-para.(6) the words "EU Tachographs Regulation" have been substituted for the words "Community Recording Equipment Regulation".

Section 99ZB. With effect from March 2, 2016, section 99ZB has been amended **A4.32** by the Passenger and Goods Vehicles (Tachographs) (Amendment) Regulations 2016 (SI 2016/248) such that the words "EU Tachographs Regulation" have been substituted for the words "Community Recording Equipment Regulation" in sub-paras (7) and (9).

A4.38   *Section 99ZE.* With effect from March 2, 2016, the following amendments have been made to section 99ZE by the Passenger and Goods Vehicles (Tachographs) (Amendment) Regulations 2016 (SI 2016/248):

1. in sub-para.(2) the words "EU Tachographs Regulation" have been substituted for the words "Community Recording Equipment Regulation";

2. in sub-para(6) the words "produces, distributes, installs, advertises or sells" have been substituted for the words "produces, supplies or installs".

A4.50   *Section 102.* With effect from July 12, 2016, the following words have been inserted at the end of sub-paragraph (4) by the Armed Forces Act 2016 (2016 c.21) s.17:

> [or for purposes relating to the functions of Ministry of Defence fire-fighters (as defined in section 16 of the Armed Forces Act 2016)]

A4.58   *Section 103.* With effect from March 2, 2016, the following amendments have been made to section 103 by the Passenger and Goods Vehicles (Tachographs) (Amendment) Regulations 2016 (SI 2016/248):

1. the definition of "the Community Recording Equipment Regulation" has been omitted;

2. the following definitions have been inserted at the appropriate place:

> ["*the EU Tachographs Regulation*" has the meaning given by section 97(7) of this Act;]
>
> ["*field test*" has the meaning given by section 96A(1) of this Act;]

3. in the definition of "*record sheet*", the words "Article 37(2) of the EU Tachographs Regulation" have been substituted for the words "Article 16(2) of the Community Recording Equipment Regulation";

4. the following sub-para has been inserted after sub-para.(9):

> [(10)   A reference in this Part of this Act to Annex IB to the EU Tachographs Regulation has effect, until the coming into force of that Annex, as a reference to Annex IB to Council Regulation (EEC) No. 3821/85 on recording equipment in road transport as read with the Community Drivers' Hours and Recording Equipment Regulations 2007.]

Road Traffic Regulations Act 1984 (1984 c.27)

A13.150   *Schedule 6, Part III.* With effect from October 1, 2015, in the table in Pt III (track-laying vehicles), the following entry has been inserted after item 5 by the Motor Vehicles (Variation of Speed Limits for Naval, Military and Air Force Vehicles) (England and Wales) Regulations 2015 (SI 2015/1653) reg.2:

[6.	A motor vehicle of a class specified in item 1 or 2 above, or in item 5 as a result of paragraph (a) of the class description of that item, which— (a) is being used for naval, military or air force purposes, (b) is being driven by persons for the time being subject to the orders of a member of the armed forces of the Crown, and (c) is being used in England or Wales.	40]

Schedule 6, Part IV. With effect from October 1, 2015, the following amend- **A13.157**
ments have been made to para.4 by the Motor Vehicles (Variation of Speed Limits
for Naval, Military and Air Force Vehicles) (England and Wales) Regulations
2015 (SI 2015/1653) reg.2:

1. the existing text becomes sub-para.(1);
2. the following sub-paragraph has been inserted after sub-para.(1):

> [(2)   A vehicle falling in the class specified in item 6 in Part III shall be
> treated as falling in that class (and not as also falling in any other class).]

Road Traffic Act 1988 (1988 c.6)

Section 5A. With effect from March 2, 2015, this section is brought into force by **A18.29**
the Drug Driving (Specified Limits) (England and Wales) Regulations 2014 (SI
2014/2868). Regulation 2 of those Regulations specifies the controlled drugs and,
in each case, the limit in blood for the purposes of the offence in s.5A of the Act,
according to the table below. The table is printed as amended by the Drug Driving (Specified Limits) (England and Wales) (Amendment) Regulations 2015 (SI
2015/911).

Controlled drug	*Limit (microgrammes per litre of blood)*
[Amphetamine	250]
Benzoylecgonine	50
Clonazepam	50
Cocaine	10
Delta-9-Tetrahydrocannabinol	2
Diazepam	550
Flunitrazepam	300
Ketamine	20
Lorazepam	100
Lysergic Acid Diethylamide	1
Methadone	500

Controlled drug	Limit (microgrammes per litre of blood)
Methylamphetamine	10
Methylenedioxymethamphetamine	10
6-Monoacetylmorphine	5
Morphine	80
Oxazepam	300
Temazepam	1000

A18.142 *Section 45.* With effect from March 2, 2016, sub-para.(8) has been amended by the Passenger and Goods Vehicles (Tachographs) (Amendment) Regulations 2016 (SI 2016/248) such that the words "EU Tachographs Regulation" have been substituted for the words "Community Recording Equipment Regulation".

A18.152 *Section 49.* With effect from March 2, 2016, sub-para.(5) has been amended by the Passenger and Goods Vehicles (Tachographs) (Amendment) Regulations 2016 (SI 2016/248) such that the words "EU Tachographs Regulation" have been substituted for the words "Community Recording Equipment Regulation".

A18.231 *Section 85.* With effect from March 2, 2016, the following amendments have been made to section 85 by the Passenger and Goods Vehicles (Tachographs) (Amendment) Regulations 2016 (SI 2016/248):

    1. the definition of "the Community Recording Equipment Regulation" has been omitted;

    2. the following definition has been inserted at the appropriate place:

      ["*the EU Tachographs Regulation*" means Regulation (EU) No. 165/2914 of the European Parliament and of the Council on tachographs in road transport as read with the Community Drivers' Hours and Recording Equipment Regulations 2007;]

A18.233 *Section 86.* With effect from March 2, 2016, the following amendments have been made to section 86 by the Passenger and Goods Vehicles (Tachographs) (Amendment) Regulations 2016 (SI 2016/248):

    1. the table entry for "Community Recording Equipment Regulation" has been omitted;

    2. after the table entry for the expression "EC certificate of conformity", the following entry has been inserted:

      [*"EU Tachographs Regulation"*   Section 85]

Road Traffic Offenders Act 1988 (1988 c.53)

Section 37. With effect from January 4, 2016, the following sub-paragraph has **A19.94** been inserted after sub-para.(3) by the Road Traffic Offenders Act 1988 and Motor Vehicles (Driving Licences) (Amendment) Regulations 2015 (SI 2015/2004):

[(4) Notwithstanding anything in Part III of the Road Traffic Act 1988, a person who holds a Community licence which authorises that person to drive motor vehicles of a particular class, but who is disqualified by an order of a court under section 36 of this Act, is (unless the person is also disqualified otherwise than by virtue of such an order) entitled to drive a motor vehicle of that class in accordance with the same conditions as if the person were authorised to drive a motor vehicle of that class by a provisional licence.]

Schedule 3. With effect from March 2, 2016, the table in Schedule 3 has been **A19.252** amended by the Passenger and Goods Vehicles (Tachographs) (Amendment) Regulations 2016 (SI 2016/248) such that, in the entry for "Section 97(1) of that Act", the words "EU Tachographs Regulation" have been substituted for the words "Community Recording Equipment Regulation".

Vehicle Excise and Registration Act 1994 (1994 c.22)

Schedule 2, para.20G. With effect from November 20, 2015, the following **A24.229** amendments have been made by the Finance (No. 2) Act 2015 (2015 c.33) s.46(3)(a):

1. the existing provision becomes sub-para.(1);
2. the following sub-paragraphs have been inserted after sub-para.(1):

[(2) But a vehicle is not an exempt vehicle by reason of this paragraph if—
   (a) it is a vehicle to which Part 1AA of Schedule 1 applies (light passenger vehicles registered on or after 1 April 2017), and
   (b) its price exceeds £40,000.
(3) Paragraph 1GF of Schedule 1 (calculating the price of a vehicle) applies for the purposes of sub-paragraph (2)(b).]

Schedule 2, para. 25. With effect from November 20, 2015, the following sub- **A24.241** paragraphs are inserted after sub-para.(3) by the Finance (No. 2) Act 2015 (2015 c.33) s.46(3)(b):

[(4) A vehicle is an exempt vehicle if—
   (a) it is a vehicle to which Part 1AA of Schedule 1 applies, and
   (b) it has an applicable CO_2 emissions figure (as defined in paragraph 1A(3) and (4) of that Schedule) of 0 g/km.
(5) But a vehicle is not an exempt vehicle by reason of subparagraph (4) if—
   (a) its price exceeds £40,000, and
   (b) less than six years have passed since it was first registered (whether under

this Act or under the law of a country or territory outside the United Kingdom).

(6) Paragraph 1GF of Schedule 1 (calculating the price of a vehicle) applies for the purposes of sub-paragraph (5)(a).]

Section B: Statutory Instruments

Road Vehicles (Construction and Use) Regulations 1986

(SI 1986/1078)

Regulation 3. With effect from March 2, 2016, the following amendments have **B15.05**
been made to the table in reg.3(2) by the Passenger and Goods Vehicles (Tachographs) (Amendment) Regulations 2016 (SI 2016/248):

1. the definition of *"the Community Recording Equipment Regulation"*
   has been omitted.

2. after the definition of *"engineering equipment"* the following definition
   has been inserted:

[*"EU Tachographs Regulation"*	Regulation (EU) No.165/2014 of the European Parliament and of the Council on tachographs in road transport as read with the Community Drivers' Hours and Recording Equipment Regulations 2007.]

Regulation 35. With effect from March 2, 2016, sub-para.(2)(h) has been **B15.77**
amended by the Passenger and Goods Vehicles (Tachographs) (Amendment)
Regulations 2016 (SI 2016/248) such that the words "EU Tachographs Regulation" have been substituted for the words "Community Recording Equipment
Regulation".

Regulation 36. With effect from March 2, 2016, sub-para.(1)(b) has been **B15.79**
amended by the Passenger and Goods Vehicles (Tachographs) (Amendment)
Regulations 2016 (SI 2016/248) such that the words "EU Tachographs Regulation" have been substituted for the words "Community Recording Equipment
Regulation".

Drivers' Hours (Goods Vehicles) (Keeping of Records) Regulations 1987

(SI 1987/1421)

Regulation 12. With effect from March 2, 2016, the following amendments have **B20.13**
been made by the Passenger and Goods Vehicles (Tachographs) (Amendment)
Regulations 2016 (SI 2016/248):

1. in sub-para.(4) the words "regulation 2(1)(b)(ii) of the Community
   Drivers' Hours and Recording Equipment Regulations 2007 (S.I. 2007/

1819) the EU Tachographs Regulation" have been substituted for the words "regulation 5 of the Community Drivers' Hours and Recording Equipment (Exemptions and Supplementary Provisions) Regulations 1986 [SI 1986/1456] Council Regulation (EEC) No.3821/85 of 20th December 1985 on recording equipment in road transport [q.v.]";

2. the following sub-para. is inserted after sub-para.(5):

[(6)   In this regulation "*the EU Tachographs Regulation*" means Regulation (EU) No. 165/2014 of the European Parliament and of the Council on tachographs in road transport.]

Zebra, Pelican and Puffin Pedestrian Crossings Regulations and General Directions 1997

(SI 1997/2400)

B36.03–
B36.94   With effect from April 22, 2016, the Regulations and Directions have been revoked by the Traffic Signs Regulations and General Directions 2016 (SI 2016/362).

The Traffic Signs (Temporary Obstructions) Regulations 1997

(SI 1997/3053)

B38.01–
B38.39   With effect from April 22, 2016, the Regulations and Directions have been revoked by the Traffic Signs Regulations and General Directions 2016 (SI 2016/362).

The Motor Vehicles (Driving Licences) Regulations 1999

(SI 1999/2864)

B43.01   *Amendments.* The text of this order has been further amended by:

the Motor Vehicles (Driving Licences) (Amendment) (No.4) Regulations 2015 (SI 2015/1797) (December 31, 2015)

the Road Traffic Offenders Act 1988 and the Motor Vehicles (Driving Licences) (Amendment) Regulations 2015 (SI 2015/2004) (January 4, 2016).

The amending order is referred to in this Noter-up only by its year and number. The date referred to is the date on which the amending order came into force.

B43.07   *Regulation 3A.* In reg.3A(1)(a), "40(2A)" has been substituted for "40(2)" and "40(2A)(a)" has been substituted for "40(2)(a)" by SI 2015/1797.

B43.43   *Regulation 43.* The following amendments have been made to reg.43 by SI 2015/1797:

1. regulation 43(5)(a)(ii) has been substituted as follows:

   [(ii) the person concerned held at the date on which he passed the test either—

       (aa) the prescribed certificate of successful completion by him of an approved training course for motor cyclists and that certificate was at that time valid in accordance with regulation 68(2), or

       (bb) a valid certificate corresponding to such a certificate which was furnished to him under the law of Northern Ireland; or]

2. regulation 43(5)(a)(iii) has been substituted as follows:

   [(iii) the person concerned holds either—

       (aa) the prescribed certificate of successful completion by him of an approved training course for motor cyclists and that certificate was furnished to him after the date on which he passed the test, and was valid in accordance with regulation 68(2) when furnished, or

       (bb) a certificate corresponding to such a certificate which was furnished to him under the law of Northern Ireland after the date on which he passed the test and was valid when so furnished, and]

Regulation 84. After reg.83, the following new regulation has been inserted by SI 2015/2004:　　　　**B43.112**

[Review

84.—(1) The Secretary of State must from time to time—

    (a) carry out a review of regulations 37 to 39 (requirements at tests),

    (b) set out the conclusions of the review in a report, and

    (c) publish the report.

(2) In carrying out the review the Secretary of State must, so far as is reasonable, have regard to how Directive 2006/126/EC of the European Parliament and of the Council on driving licences (which is implemented in part by means of these Regulations) is implemented in other member States.

(3) The report must in particular—

    (a) set out the objectives intended to be achieved by the regulatory system established by these Regulations,

    (b) assess the extent to which those objectives are achieved, and

    (c) assess whether those objectives remain appropriate and, if so, the extent to which they could be achieved with a system that impose less regulation.

(4) The first report under this regulation must be published before the 4th January 2021.

(5) Reports under this regulation are afterward to be published at intervals not exceeding five years.]

Noter–up to Volume 2

The Road Vehicles (Registration and Licensing) Regulations 2002

(SI 2002/2742)

B51.01 *Amendments.* The text of this order has been further amended by:

the Road Vehicles (Registration and Licensing) (Amendment) (No. 2)
Regulations 2015 (SI 2015/1657) (October 1, 2015).

The amending order is referred to in this Noter-up only by its year and number.
The date referred to is the date on which the amending order came into force.

B51.19 *Regulation 13.* In reg.13(3), the words "regulations 15 and 15A" have been substituted for the words "regulation 15" by SI 2015/1657.

B51.21 *Regulation 14.* In reg.14(4)(c), the words "regulations 15 and 15A" have been substituted for the words "regulation 15" by SI 2015/1657.

B51.23 *Regulation 15.* The following amendments have been made to reg.15 by SI 2015/ 1657:

1. in reg.15(1), the words "Unless regulation 15A applies, before" have been substituted for the word "Before".
2. in reg.15(1A), the words "Unless regulation 15A applies, before" have been substituted for the word "Before".
3. reg.15(3) has been substituted as follows:

[(3)   Unless paragraph (3B) applies, the provisions of Schedule 3 shall have effect in relation to the issue of a new registration document in respect of a vehicle (in this regulation and in Schedule 3 called "*the relevant vehicle*") where paragraph (3A) applies.]

4. After reg.15(3), as substituted, the following new paragraphs have been inserted:

(3A) [This paragraph applies where—
   (a) the relevant vehicle falls within the category M1 described in paragraph 1.1.1. of Annex II to Directive 2007/46/EC of the European Parliament and of the Council establishing a framework for the approval of motor vehicles and their trailers, and of systems, components and separate units intended for such vehicles; and
   (b) either an insurer has informed the Secretary of State that it has decided to pay the pre-accident value of the relevant vehicle to the owner in preference to paying for is less than the cost of repairing it or the registration document has been surrendered to the Secretary of State under regulation 20(5).

(3B) This paragraph applies if—
   (a) the relevant vehicle is a vehicle described in paragraph (3A);
   (b) the insurer or the keeper of a fleet has notified the Secretary of State that the relevant vehicle is suitable for repair; and

(c) the request for a new registration document is made on or after 1st October 2015 but before 26th October 2015.

(3C) If paragraph (3B) applies, the Secretary of State must treat the request for a new registration document as made under regulation 15A except that paragraph (1) of that regulation is disapplied.]

5. After reg.15(3C), as inserted, the following new regulation has been inserted:

[Note. The insertion at para.(3A)(b) appears incomplete. No further amendment or addition has been published to date.]

[Issue of new registration document from 26th October 2015

15A.—(1) This regulation applies where a request for a new registration document is made on or after 26th October 2015.

(2) Before issuing a new registration document in respect of a vehicle under any provision of these Regulations, the Secretary of State may require the keeper of the vehicle to satisfy him by the production of the vehicle or other sufficient evidence that the vehicle—

(a) accords with the particulars furnished when a vehicle or nil licence was last applied for in respect of it; or

(b) is the registered vehicle.

(3) Before issuing a new registration document the Secretary of State may take actions to satisfy himself that the identity and address of the person seeking to be the registered keeper accords with the information given to him.

(4) The Secretary of State may refuse to issue a new registration document in respect of a vehicle if he is not satisfied as mentioned in paragraphs (2) and (3).

(5) The provisions of Schedule 3A shall have effect in relation to the issue of a new registration document in respect of a vehicle (in this regulation and in Schedule 3A called *"the relevant vehicle"*) where the relevant vehicle falls within a category described in paragraph (6) and one of the conditions in paragraph (7) is satisfied.

(6) The categories of vehicle are—

(a) M1 and N1 described in paragraph 1.1.1. and 1.2.1. respectively of Annex II to Directive 2007/46/EC of the European Parliament and of the Council establishing a framework for the approval of motor vehicles and their trailers, and of systems, components and separate technical units intended for such vehicles; and

(b) L1e to L7e described in Annex 1 to Regulation (EU) 168/2013 of the European Parliament and of the Council on the approval and market surveillance of two or three-wheel vehicles and quadricycles.

(7) The conditions are that—

(a) an insurer has informed the Secretary of State that the pre-accident value of the relevant vehicle is less than the cost of repairing it;

(b) the registration document has been surrendered to the Secretary of State under regulation 20(5) (change of keeper: general provisions);

(c) the keeper of a fleet has informed the Secretary of State that the relevant vehicle has not been insured with an insurer and the pre-accident value of the vehicle is less than the cost of repairing it.]

B51.25 *Regulation 16.* In reg.16(4)(b), the words "regulations 15 and 15A" have been substituted for the words "regulation 15" by SI 2015/1657.

B51.31 *Regulation 18.* In reg.18(2)(b), the words "regulations 15 and 15A" have been substituted for the words "regulation 15" by SI 2015/1657.

B51.35 *Regulation 20.* In reg.20(3), the words "and 15A" have been inserted after the number "15" by SI 2015/1657.

B51.38 *Regulation 22.* In reg.22(5)(b), the words "regulations 15 and 15A" have been substituted for the words "regulation 15" by SI 2015/1657.

B51.42 *Regulation 24.* In reg.24(8)(b), the words "regulations 15 and 15A" have been substituted for the words "regulation 15" by SI 2015/1657.

B51.51 *Regulation 30.* In reg.30(5)(a), "15A," has been inserted after "15" by SI 2015/1657.

B51.72 *Regulation 47.* After reg.47, the following new regulation has been inserted by SI 2015/1657:

[Review

48.—(1) The Secretary of State must from time to time carry out a review of the provisions listed in paragraph (2).

(2) The listed provisions are—

(a) regulation 15(1) and (3) to (3C) (issue of a new registration document before 26th October 2015);

(b) regulation 15A (issue of a new registration document from 26th October); and

(c) Schedule 3A (duties of the insurer, keeper and Secretary of State in relation to the issue of a new registration document from 26th October).

(3) The Secretary of State must—

(a) set out the conclusions of the review carried out in accordance with paragraph (1) in a report; and

(b) publish the report.

(4) The report must in particular—

(a) set out the objectives intended to be achieved by the regulatory system established by those provisions;

(b) assess the extent to which those objectives are achieved; and

(c) assess whether those objectives remain appropriate and, if so, the extent to which they could be achieved with a system that imposes less regulation.

(5) The first report under this regulation must be published before the end of the period of five years beginning with the day on which the provisions listed under paragraph (2) come into force.

(6) Reports under this regulation are afterwards to be published at intervals not exceeding five years.]

Schedule 3. After Sch.3(8) the following new schedule has been inserted by SI 2015/1657: **B51.81**

[**Regulation 15A**   SCHEDULE 3A

ISSUE OF NEW REGISTRATION DOCUMENT FROM 26ᴛʜ OCTOBER 2015

Duty of the insurer

1.—(1) I an insurer determines that the relevant vehicle for which it provides a policy of insurance has sustained damage such that the repair costs including value added tax exceed the pre-accident value of that vehicle—

(a) that insurer must notify the Secretary of State whether the relevant vehicle is suitable for repair or not as the case may be; and

(b) unless that insurer is also the keeper of the relevant vehicle, the insurer must notify the keeper of that vehicle—

(i) that the vehicle repair costs including value added tax exceed the pre-accident value of that vehicle, and

(ii) if the vehicle is suitable for repair or not as the case may be.

(2) Following notification in accordance with paragraph (1)(a) the insurer must destroy the registration document if this is in its possession.

Duty of the keeper

2.—(1) Where a keeper of a fleet is the keeper of a relevant vehicle that is not insured with an insurer and the pre-accident value of the vehicle is less than the cost of repairing it, that keeper must—

(a) notify the Secretary of State if—

(i) the vehicle has sustained damage, and

(ii) the vehicle is suitable for repair; and

(b) destroy the registration document for that vehicle.

(2) Where the keeper of a relevant vehicle receives a notification from an insurer in accordance with paragraph 1(1)(b), that keeper must forthwith surrender the registration document for that vehicle to the Secretary of State unless that document is held by the insurer.

Application for a new registration document

3. The keeper of a relevant vehicle may apply for a new registration document for that vehicle if—

(a) an insurer has determined that the relevant vehicle is suitable for repair; or

(b) the application is made by the keeper of a fleet who has notified the Secretary of State in accordance with paragraph 2(1)(a) that the relevant vehicle is suitable for repair.

Duty of the Secretary of State

4. Where the keeper of a vehicle applies for a new registration document under paragraph 3, that keeper may be required to provide in relation to the vehicle such other evidence as the Secretary of State may specify.

Determination by the Secretary of State

5. The Secretary of State must issue a new registration document or notify the applicant if a new registration document is not issued after considering any notification given by the insurer under paragraph 1(1)(a) or a keeper of a fleet under paragraph 2(1)(a)(ii) as to whether the vehicle is suitable for repair.

Registration document

6. Where the Secretary of State is satisfied that a new registration document may be issued for the relevant vehicle, the Secretary of State must issue a new registration document.]

The Traffic Signs Regulations and General Directions 2002

(SI 2002/3113)

B53.03–
B53.296 With effect from April 22, 2016, the Regulations and Directions have been revoked by the Traffic Signs Regulations and General Directions 2016 (SI 2016/362).

The Passenger and Goods Vehicles (Recording Equipment) (Tachograph Card) Regulations 2006

(SI 2006/1937)

B57.03 *Regulation 2.* With effect from March 2, 2016, the following amendments have been made by the Passenger and Goods Vehicles (Tachographs) (Amendment) Regulations 2016 (SI 2016/248):

    1. the existing text becomes sub-para.(1);

    2. in that sub-para, the definition of *"the Community Recording Equipment Regulation"* is omitted;

    3. in that sub-para, in the definition of *"company card"*, *"control card"*, *"driver card"* and *"workshop card"* the words "Article 2 of the EU Tachographs Regulation" are substituted for the words "Annex 1B to the Community Recording Equipment Regulation";

    4. in that sub-para, after the entry for *"company card"* etc, the following definition is inserted:

        [*"the EU Tachographs Regulation"* means Regulation (EU) No. 165/2014 of the European Parliament and of the Council on tachographs in road transport as read with the Community Drivers' Hours and Recording Equipment Regulations 2007."]

    5. After sub-para.(1), the following new sub-para.has been inserted:

[(2)   A reference in these Regulations to Annex IB to the EU Tachographs Regulation has effect, until the coming into force of that Annex, as a reference to Annex IB to Council Regulation (EEC) No. 3821/85 on recording equipment in road transport as read with the Community Drivers' Hours and Recording Equipment Regulations 2007.]

The Community Drivers' Hours and Recording Equipment Regulations 2007

(SI 2007/1819)

Regulation 1. With effect from March 2, 2016, sub-para.(2) has been amended by the Passenger and Goods Vehicles (Tachographs) (Amendment) Regulations 2016 (SI 2016/248) such that the words ""*the EU Tachographs Regulation*" means Regulation (EU) No. 165/2014 of the European Parliament and of the Council on tachographs in road transport" are substituted for the words ""*the Community Recording Equipment Regulation*" means Council Regulation (EEC) No. 3821/85".

B59.02

Regulation 2. With effect from March 2, 2016, sub-para.(1)(b)(iii) has been amended by the Passenger and Goods Vehicles (Tachographs) (Amendment) Regulations 2016 (SI 2016/248) such that the number "100" has been substituted for the number "50".

B59.03

Regulation 4. With effect from March 2, 2016, the heading and sub-paras (1) and (2) have been amended by the Passenger and Goods Vehicles (Tachographs) (Amendment) Regulations 2016 (SI 2016/248) such that the words "EU Tachographs Regulation" have been substituted for the words "Community Recording Equipment Regulation" .

B59.05

Schedule. With effect from March 2, 2016, the following amendments have been made by the Passenger and Goods Vehicles (Tachographs) (Amendment) Regulations 2016 (SI 2016/248):

**B59.11,
B59.13,
B59.22**

1. para.4 is omitted;
2. in para.6 "100" is substituted for "50";
3. in para. 15 "100" is substituted for "50".

Section C: European Union Legislation

Regulation (EC) 1073/2009 of October 21, 2009 on common rules for access to the international market for coach and bus services, and amending Regulation (EC) 561/2006

C12.02   *Amendments.* The text of this Regulation has been further amended by:

> Corrigendum to Regulation (EC) No 1073/2009 of the European Parliament and of the Council of 21 October 2009 on common rules for access to the international market for coach and bus services, and amending Regulation (EC) No 561/2006 (Official Journal of the European Union L 300 of 14 November 2009) (O.J. No L272, October 16, 2015 p.15).

C12.06   *Article 5.* With effect from October 16, 2015, art. 5(2) is amended such that the words "in particular" have been inserted after the words "shall include".

Regulation (EU) 165/2014 of the European Parliament and of the Council of 4 February 2014 on tachographs in road transport

C13.01   *[This Regulation is implemented and supplemented by Commission Implementing Regulation (EU) 2016/799 of 18 March 2016 implementing Regulation (EU) No 165/2014 of the European Parliament and of the Council laying down the requirements for the construction, testing, installation, operation and repair of tachographs and their components, which is not included in this work for reasons of scale but which may be found at http://eur-lex.europa.eu/legal-content/EN/TXT/?qid=1471865948873&uri=CELEX:32016R0799 [accessed August 22, 2016]]*

Legislation

Section B: Statutory Instruments

Criminal Procedure Rules 2015

(SI 2015/1490)

ARRANGEMENT OF REGULATIONS

B70.01   Preamble

* * *

PART 29

ROAD TRAFFIC PENALTIES

* * *

PREAMBLE

Preamble

B70.02   The Criminal Procedure Rule Committee—

(a) revokes the Criminal Procedure Rules 2014 and makes the following Rules under section 69 of the Courts Act 2003, after consulting in accordance with section 72(1)(a) of that Act; and

(b) *[Omitted]*.

These Rules may be cited as the Criminal Procedure Rules 2015 and shall come into force on 5th October 2015.

* * *

PART 29

ROAD TRAFFIC PENALTIES

29.1.—(1) This rule applies— **B70.03**

(a) where the court—

    (i) convicts the defendant of an offence involving obligatory disqualification from driving and section 34(1) of the Road Traffic Offenders Act 1988 (Disqualification for certain offences) applies,

    (ii) convicts the defendant of an offence where section 35 of the 1988 Act (Disqualification for repeated offences) applies, or

    (iii) convicts the defendant of an offence involving obligatory endorsement of the defendant's driving record and section 44 of the 1988 Act (Orders for endorsement) applies;

(b) unless the defendant is absent.

(2) The court must explain, in terms the defendant can understand (with help, if necessary)—

(a) where paragraph (1)(a)(i) applies (obligatory disqualification under section 34)—

    (i) that the court must order the defendant to be disqualified from driving for a minimum of 12 months (or 2 or 3 years, as the case may be, according to the offence and the defendant's driving record), unless the court decides that there are special reasons to order disqualification for a shorter period, or not to order disqualification at all, and

    (ii) if applicable, that the period of disqualification will be reduced by at least 3 months if, by no later than 2 months before the end of the reduced period, the defendant completes an approved driving course;

(b) where paragraph (1)(a)(ii) applies (disqualification under section 35)—

    (i) that the court must order the defendant to be disqualified from driving for a minimum of 6 months (or 1 or 2 years, as the case may be, according to the defendant's driving record), unless, having regard to all the circumstances, the court decides to order disqualification for a shorter period, or not to order disqualification at all, and

    (ii) that circumstances of which the court cannot take account in making its decision are any that make the offence not a serious

89

one; hardship (other than exceptional hardship); and any that during the last 3 years already have been taken into account by a court when ordering disqualification for less than the usual minimum period, or not at all, for repeated driving offences;

(c) where paragraph (1)(a)(iii) applies (obligatory endorsement), that the court must order the endorsement of the defendant's driving record unless the court decides that there are special reasons not to do so;

(d) in every case, as applicable—

(i) that the court already has received representations from the defendant about whether any such special reasons or mitigating circumstances apply and will take account of them, or

(ii) that the defendant may make such representations now, on oath or affirmation.

(3) Unless the court already has received such representations from the defendant, before it applies rule 24.11 (magistrates' court procedure if the court convicts) or rule 25.16 (Crown Court procedure if the court convicts), as the case may be, the court must—

(a) ask whether the defendant wants to make any such representations; and

(b) if the answer to that question is 'yes', require the defendant to take an oath or affirm and make them.

B70.04 *[Note. For the circumstances in which the court —*

(a) may, and in some cases must, order disqualification from driving under the Road Traffic Offenders Act 1988, see ss.26, 34, 35 and 36 of that Act;

(b) may, for some reasons or in some circumstances, abbreviate or dispense with a period of disqualification otherwise required by the 1988 Act, see ss.34(1) and 35(1), (4) of that Act;

(c) must usually order endorsement, see ss.9, 44 and 96 of, and Sch. 2 to, the 1988 Act.

For the circumstances in which the period of a disqualification from driving will be reduced if the defendant completes an approved driving course, see s.34A of the 1988 Act .]

Application to remove a disqualification from driving

B70.05 **29.2.**—(1) This rule applies where, on application by the defendant, the court can remove a disqualification from driving.

(2) A defendant who wants the court to exercise that power must—

(a) apply in writing, no earlier than the date on which the court can exercise the power;

(b) serve the application on the court officer; and

(c) in the application—

    (i) specify the disqualification, and

    (ii) explain why the defendant wants the court to remove it.

(3) The court officer must serve a copy of the application on the chief officer of police for the local justice area.

[Note. For the circumstances in which the court may remove a disqualification **B70.06** *from driving imposed under s.34 or 35 of the Road Traffic Offenders Act 1988, see s.42 of the Act. The court may not consider an application made within two years of the disqualification, in any case; or, after that, before a specified period has expired.]*

Information to be supplied on order for endorsement of driving record, etc.

29.3.—(1) This rule applies where the court—   **B70.07**

    (a) convicts the defendant of an offence involving obligatory endorsement, and orders there to be endorsed on the defendant's driving record (and on any counterpart licence, if other legislation requires)—

        (i) particulars of the conviction,

        (ii) particulars of any disqualification from driving that the court imposes, and

        (iii) the penalty points to be attributed to the offence;

    (b) disqualifies the defendant from driving for any other offence; or

    (c) suspends or removes a disqualification from driving.

(2) The court officer must, as soon as practicable, serve on the Secretary of State notice that includes details of—

    (a) where paragraph (1)(a) applies—

        (i) the local justice area in which the court is acting,

        (ii) the dates of conviction and sentence,

        (iii) the offence, and the date on which it was committed,

        (iv) the sentence, and

        (v) the date of birth, and sex, of the defendant, where those details are available;

    (b) where paragraph (1)(b) applies—

        (i) the date and period of the disqualification,

        (ii) the power exercised by the court;

    (c) where paragraph (1)(c) applies—

        (i) the date and period of the disqualification,

        (ii) the date and terms of the order for its suspension or removal,

        (iii) the power exercised by the court, and

        (iv) where the court suspends the disqualification pending appeal, the court to which the defendant has appealed.

B70.08 *[Note. See ss.39(3), 42(5), 44A, 47 and 97A of the Road Traffic Offenders Act 1988.*

Under s.25 of the 1988 Act, the court may order a defendant to disclose his or her date of birth, and sex, where that is not apparent (for example, where the defendant is convicted in his or her absence). Under s.27 of the 1988 Act, and under ss.146(4) and 147(5) of the Powers of Criminal Courts (Sentencing) Act 2000, the court may order a defendant to produce his or her driving licence, if not already produced.

For the circumstances in which the court —

    (a) must usually order endorsement, see ss.9, 44 and 96 of, and Sch. 2 to, the 1988 Act;

    (b) may, and in some cases must, order disqualification from driving under the 1988 Act, see ss.26, 34, 35 and 36 of that Act;

    (c) may order disqualification from driving under the 2000 Act, see ss.146 and 147 of that Act;

    (d) may suspend a disqualification from driving pending appeal, see ss.39 and 40 of the 1988 Act (Pt 34 (Appeal to the Crown Court) and Pt 35 (Appeal to the High Court by case stated) contain relevant rules);

    (e) may remove a disqualification from driving imposed under s.34 or 35 of the 1988 Act, see s.42 of that Act (r.29.2 applies).]

Statutory declaration to avoid fine after fixed penalty notice

B70.09 **29.4.**—(1) This rule applies where—

    (a) a chief officer of police, or the Secretary of State, serves on the magistrates' court officer a certificate registering, for enforcement as a fine, a sum payable by a defendant after failure to comply with a fixed penalty notice;

    (b) the court officer notifies the defendant of the registration; and

    (c) the defendant makes a statutory declaration with the effect that there become void—

        (i) the fixed penalty notice, or any associated notice sent to the defendant as owner of the vehicle concerned, and

        (ii) the registration and any enforcement proceedings.

(2) The defendant must serve that statutory declaration not more than 21 days after service of notice of the registration, unless the court extends that time limit.

(3) The court officer must—

    (a) serve a copy of the statutory declaration on the person by whom the certificate was registered;

    (b) cancel any endorsement on the defendant's driving record (and on any counterpart licence, if other legislation requires); and

    (c) notify the Secretary of State of any such cancellation.

B70.10 *[Note. See ss.72(1), (6), (6A), 73(1) and 74(2) of the Road Traffic Offenders Act 1988.*

For the circumstances in which —

    (a) a sum may be registered for enforcement as a fine after failure to comply with a fixed penalty notice, see ss.54, 55, 62, 63, 64, 70 and 71 of the 1988 Act;

    (b) the registration may become void on the making of a statutory declaration by the defendant, see ss.72 and 73 of the 1988 Act.]

Application for declaration about a course or programme certificate decision

29.5.—(1) This rule applies where the court can declare unjustified—   **B70.11**

    (a) a course provider's failure or refusal to give a certificate of the defendant's satisfactory completion of an approved course; or

    (b) a programme provider's giving of a certificate of the defendant's failure fully to participate in an approved programme.

(2) A defendant who wants the court to exercise that power must—

    (a) apply in writing, not more than 28 days after—

        (i) the date by which the defendant was required to complete the course, or

        (ii) the giving of the certificate of failure fully to participate in the programme;

    (b) serve the application on the court officer; and

    (c) in the application, specify the course or programme and explain (as applicable)—

        (i) that the course provider has failed to give a certificate,

        (ii) where the course provider has refused to give a certificate, why the defendant disagrees with the reasons for that decision, or

        (iii) where the programme provider has given a certificate, why the defendant disagrees with the reasons for that decision.

(3) The court officer must serve a copy of the application on the course or programme provider.

(4) The court must not determine the application unless the defendant, and the course or programme provider, each has had an opportunity to make representations at a hearing (whether or not either in fact attends).

[Note. For the circumstances in which the court may reduce a road traffic   **B70.12** *penalty on condition that the defendant attend an approved course, or take part in an approved programme, see ss.30A, 34A and 34D of the Road Traffic Offenders Act 1988.*

    Under ss.30B, 34B and 34E of the 1988 Act, the court that made the order, or the defendant's local magistrates' court, on application by the defendant may review a course or programme provider's decision that the defendant has not completed the course satisfactorily, or has not participated fully in the programme.]

Appeal against recognition of foreign driving disqualification

B70.13   **29.6.**—(1) This rule applies where—

(a) a Minister gives a disqualification notice under section 57 of the Crime (International Co-operation) Act 2003; and

(b) the person to whom it is given wants to appeal under section 59 of the Act to a magistrates' court.

(2) That person ('the appellant') must serve an appeal notice on—

(a) the court officer, at a magistrates' court in the local justice area in which the appellant lives; and

(b) the Minister, at the address given in the disqualification notice.

(3) The appellant must serve the appeal notice within the period for which section 59 of the 2003 Act provides.

(4) The appeal notice must—

(a) attach a copy of the disqualification notice;

(b) explain which of the conditions in section 56 of the 2003 Act is not met, and why section 57 of the Act therefore does not apply; and

(c) include any application to suspend the disqualification, under section 60 of the Act.

(5) The Minister may serve a respondent's notice, and must do so if—

(a) the Minister wants to make representations to the court; or

(b) the court so directs.

(6) The Minister must—

(a) unless the court otherwise directs, serve any such respondent's notice not more than 14 days after—

(i) the appellant serves the appeal notice, or

(ii) a direction to do so;

(b) in any such respondent's notice—

(i) identify the grounds of opposition on which the Minister relies,

(ii) summarise any relevant facts not already included in the disqualification and appeal notices, and

(iii) identify any other document that the Minister thinks the court will need to decide the appeal (and serve any such document with the notice).

(7) Where the court determines an appeal, the general rule is that it must do so at a hearing (which must be in public, unless the court otherwise directs).

(8) The court officer must serve on the Minister—

(a) notice of the outcome of the appeal;

(b) notice of any suspension of the disqualification; and

(c) the appellant's driving licence, if surrendered to the court officer.

[Note. Section 56 of the Crime (International Co-operation) Act 2003 sets out **B70.14** *the conditions for recognition in the United Kingdom of a foreign driving disqualification, and provides that s.57 of the Act applies where they are met. Under s.57, the appropriate Minister may, and in some cases must, give the person concerned notice that he or she is disqualified in the UK, too, and for what period.*

Under s.59 of the 2003 Act, that person may appeal to a magistrates' court. If the court is satisfied that s.57 of the Act does not apply in that person's case, the court must allow the appeal and notify the Minister. Otherwise, it must dismiss the appeal.

The time limit for appeal under s.59 of the 2003 Act is the end of the period of 21 days beginning with the day on which the Minister gives the notice under s.57. That period may be neither extended nor shortened.

Under s.60 of the 2003 Act, the court may suspend the disqualification, on such terms as it thinks fit.

Under s.63 of the 2003 Act, it is an offence for a person to whom the Minister gives a notice under s.57 not to surrender any licence that he or she holds, within the same period as for an appeal.]

* * *

Traffic Signs Regulations and General Directions 2016

(SI 2016/362)

ARRANGEMENT OF REGULATIONS

B71.01

PART 1

* * *

95

PART 1

THE TRAFFIC SIGNS REGULATIONS 2016

Citation, commencement and extent

B71.02   **1.** *[Omitted.]*

Interpretation

B71.03   **2.**—(1) In these Regulations—

(a) *"the 1984 Act"* means the Road Traffic Regulation Act 1984; and

96

(b) *"the 1988 Act"* means the Road Traffic Act 1988.

(2) Schedule 1 contains other definitions.

Prescription of signs

3.—(1) A traffic sign for conveying a warning, information, requirement, restriction or prohibition of a description specified in these Regulations is of a prescribed size, colour and type if it complies with all applicable requirements provided for in these Regulations.

B71.04

(2) A school crossing patrol sign is a prescribed sign within the meaning of section 28(4) of the 1984 Act if it complies with all applicable requirements as to size, colour and type provided for in these Regulations.

(3) The Parts of a Schedule specified in column 2 of an item in the table contain provisions about signs of the class specified in column 3 of the item.

(1)	*(2)*	*(3)*
Item	*Schedule*	*Purpose of nature of signs*
1	Schedule 2 Parts 1 to 7	Signs that warn of hazards and signs for bridges and other structures
2	Schedule 3 Parts 1 to 4	Upright signs that indicate regulatory requirements for moving traffic
3	Schedule 4 Parts 1 to 5	Upright signs that control waiting, loading and parking along a road
4	Schedule 5 Parts 1 to 4	Signs that indicate parking places and areas subject to parking controls
5	Schedule 6 Parts 1 and 2	Upright signs for red routes
6	Schedule 7 Parts 1 to 6	Road markings and miscellaneous upright signs that indicate stopping, waiting, loading and parking controls
7	Schedule 8 Parts 1 to 4	Signs indicating the entrance to and the end of, a pedestrian, or pedestrian and cycle, zone, and signs for charging schemes
8	Schedule 9 Parts 1 to 8	Regulatory signs at junctions and miscellaneous regulatory signs
9	Schedule 10 Parts 1 to 3	Signs for speed limits
10	Schedule 11 Parts 1 to 6	Signs that give information, are advisory or guide traffic

(1)	*(2)*	*(3)*
Item	*Schedule*	*Purpose of nature of signs*
11	Schedule 12 Parts 1 to 28	Directional signs
12	Schedule 13 Parts 1 to 11	Signs only for use in temporary situations
13	Schedule 14 Parts 1 to 5	Signs for traffic control by light signals, signs for crossings, and signs for lane control
14	Schedule 15 Parts 1 to 4	Matrix signs and light signals for the control of moving traffic on motorways and dual carriageway roads
15	Schedule 16 Parts 1 to 7	Variable message signs

(4) Where in these Regulations provision is made that to convey a warning, information, requirement, restriction or prohibition of a description specified, a sign must comply with certain requirements as to size, colour and type, that provision is without prejudice to different requirements elsewhere in the Regulations in relation to the same description.

Authorisations

B71.05 **4.** Nothing in these Regulations limits a power of the Secretary of State, the Scottish Ministers or the Welsh Ministers to authorise a sign under section 28(4) or 64 of the 1984 Act.

Letters, numerals and other characters

B71.06 **5.**—(1) This regulation applies to the letters, numerals and other characters used on signs provided for in these Regulations (but not to the extent that more specific provision is made elsewhere in these Regulations for a particular sign).

(2) Paragraphs (3) to (12) apply to letters, numerals and other characters used on signs except those used on road markings and those used in Scottish Gaelic words or phrases.

(3) Paragraphs (4) to (10) are subject to the exception for variable message signs at paragraphs (11) and (12).

(4) On a background which is—

(a) black;

(b) blue;

(c) brown;

(d) dark green;

(e) green; or

(f) red,

letters, numerals and other characters must have the proportions and form, and be of the colour, shown in Part 1 of Schedule 17 (see paragraphs (6) to (8) for exceptions).

(5) On a background which is—

(a) orange;

(b) white; or

(c) yellow,

letters, numerals and other characters must have the proportions and form, and be of the colour, shown in Part 2 of Schedule 17 (see paragraph (10) for an exception).

(6) Paragraphs (7) and (8) apply to the placing of a motorway route number or a compass point directly on the blue background shown at item 1 of the sign table at Part 2 of Schedule 12 (see paragraph (9) for an exception).

(7) Where brackets are not used, the letters, numerals and other characters must have the proportions and form, and be of the colour, shown in Part 3 of Schedule 17.

(8) Where brackets are used the letters, numerals and other characters must have the proportions and form, and be of the colour, shown in either Part 1 or Part 3 of Schedule 17.

(9) An exception to paragraphs (7) and (8) is that where the route number or compass point is part of a legend provided for at item 8 of the sign table in Part 3 of Schedule 12, letters, numerals and other characters must have the proportions and form, and be of the colour, shown in Part 1 of Schedule 17.

(10) When used for indicating a route number or compass point on a sign with a yellow background which is temporarily placed on a motorway, letters, numerals and other characters must have the proportions and form, and be of the colour, shown in Part 4 of Schedule 17.

(11) Paragraph (12) applies to a variable message sign where the construction or method of operation of the sign does not permit the use of letters, numerals and other characters of the proportions and form shown in Part 1, 2, 3 or 4 of Schedule 17.

(12) Letters, numerals and other characters may have the proportions and form shown in Part 5 of Schedule 17 (and be of the colour provided for in Part 1, 2, 3 or 4 as applicable).

(13) Paragraph (14) applies to letters, numerals and other characters incorporated in road markings provided for in these Regulations.

(14) A letter, numeral or other character of a height referred to in column 1 of the table in this paragraph must have the proportions and form, and be of the colour, shown in the Part of Schedule 17 at the column 2 entry applicable to that height.

Height of letters, numerals and other characters	Applicable Part in Schedule 17
from 280 mm to 700 mm (inclusive)	Part 6
705 mm, 1035 mm, 1600 mm	Part 7
2800 mm	Part 8

(15) For the purposes of interpreting Part 7 of Schedule 17 where the road marking is 705 mm or 1035 mm, the reference in the diagram in Part 7 to *"1600"* is to be read as *"705"* or *"1035"* as appropriate and the spaces between the grid lines reduced proportionately.

(16) Letters, numerals and other characters used in Scottish Gaelic words or phrases—

(a) when appearing on a brown or dark green background, must have the proportions and form, and be of the colour, shown in Part 9 of Schedule 17;

(b) when appearing on a white background, must have the proportions and form, and be of the colour, shown in Part 10 of Schedule 17.

(17) In Schedule 17, in Parts 1 to 4, 9 and 10, the height of the rectangular backgrounds on which the letters, numerals and other characters are shown is eight stroke widths.

Expressions of time and distance and for parking restrictions

B71.07   **6.**—(1) A reference in these Regulations to the inclusion on a sign of a *"time period"* means the inclusion of a period of time that complies with the requirements of Part 1 of Schedule 18.

(2) More than one period of time may be included in a sign if appropriate for conveying the meaning of the sign.

(3) A reference in these Regulations to the inclusion on a sign of a *"permitted parking expression"* means the inclusion of an expression that complies with the requirements of Part 2 of Schedule 18.

(4) An expression of distance on a sign must be in imperial units and comply with the requirements of Part 3 of Schedule 18.

(5) The provisions of this regulation do not apply where more specific provision in relation to a particular sign is made elsewhere in these Regulations.

Dimensions and design of signs

B71.08   **7.**—(1) This regulation is about the measurements specified in the Schedules for dimensions of signs, and elements of signs, and about overall design of signs provided for in these Regulations.

(2) All measurements specified in a diagram in the Schedules are in millimetres ("mm") unless stated otherwise or the context requires otherwise.

(3) If more than one measurement is specified for the same dimension, any of those measurements may be used for that dimension.

(4) If minimum and maximum measurements are specified for a dimension, the dimension used must not be less than the minimum or more than the maximum.

(5) Dimensions chosen for each element of a sign must correspond with one another so that the overall shape and proportions of the sign are, so far as reasonably practicable, as shown in the diagram, or as otherwise provided for, in the Schedules.

(6) The requirement at paragraph (5) does not apply to the signs provided for at—

(a) items 5, 6, and 7 of the sign table in Part 4 of Schedule 7;

(b) items 5, 12 and 13 of the sign table in Part 6 of Schedule 9;

(c) items 23, 25, 27 and 36 of the sign table in Part 4 of Schedule 11; and

(d) items 32, 33, 34, 48, 49, 50, 52, 53, 55, 56 and 57 of the sign table in Part 2 of Schedule 14.

(7) Any dimension given in millimetres in respect of a sign, other than a road marking, is to be treated as permitted if it is varied, to be either greater or less than the dimension given, by up to 5 mm.

(8) Paragraph (7) does not permit a dimension to be less than a specified minimum nor more than a specified maximum, except where the dimension relates to the height of letters, numerals or other characters.

(9) Any dimension (not being specified as a maximum or minimum) given for a road marking is to be treated as permitted if it is varied in accordance with the following table.

(1)	(2)	(3)
Item	Dimensions shown in road marking diagram	Permitted variations
1	3 metres or more	(i) Up to 15% of the dimension where the varied dimension is greater than the specified dimension; or (ii) Up to 10% of the dimension where the varied dimension is less than the specified dimension

(1)	(2)	(3)
Item	Dimensions shown in road marking diagram	Permitted variations
2	300 mm or more, but less than 3 metres	(i) Up to 20% of the dimension where the varied dimension is greater than the specified dimension; or (ii) Up to 10% of the dimension where the varied dimension is less than the specified dimension
3	Less than 300 mm	(i) Up to 30% of the dimension where the varied dimension is greater than the specified dimension; or (ii) Up to 10% of the dimension where the varied dimension is less than the specified dimension

(10) Where a dimension denoting the length or width of a road marking is varied in accordance with paragraph (9), and there is a space between two parts of the marking, the dimensions of that space may be varied as required to accommodate the variation of the length or width of the marking, provided that the character of the marking is maintained.

(11) Where the dimensions of a signal which displays an arrow or symbol are varied in accordance with paragraph (7), the dimensions chosen for the arrow or symbol must maintain the shape and proportions shown in the diagram in which the signal is shown.

(12) Any variation of any angle is to be treated as permitted if the variation does not exceed 5 degrees.

(13) Paragraph (12) does not permit an angle which is less than the minimum, or greater than the maximum, given.

(14) Where—

    (a) overall dimensions are given for a sign (other than a road marking); and

    (b) the sign displays a legend or symbol which is varied or added in accordance with these Regulations,

the overall dimensions, the number of lines filled by the legend, or both, may be varied so far as necessary to give effect to the variation or addition.

(15) Where these Regulations provide for a sign to be made up of a number of elements (including legends) but do not indicate where those elements are to be placed on the sign, regard is to be had, when deciding where to place those elements, to the purpose of the sign, in particular the nature of the message to be conveyed.

Illumination of upright signs and associated plates

8.—(1) Paragraph (2) applies to an upright sign unless elsewhere in these Regulations in relation to a particular sign— **B71.09**

    (a) requirements are imposed as to the illumination of the sign; or

    (b) provision is made that the sign need not be illuminated.

(2) The upright sign must be—

    (a) illuminated throughout the hours of darkness by internal or external lighting; or

    (b) reflectorised.

(3) If provision is made elsewhere in these Regulations that an upright sign need not be illuminated, it may be illuminated in accordance with paragraph (5).

(4) Paragraph (5) also applies to an upright sign which must at certain times be illuminated under these Regulations during those times when it is not required to be illuminated.

(5) The upright sign may be—

    (a) illuminated by internal or external lighting; or

    (b) reflectorised.

(6) Where these Regulations provide for a choice of methods of illumination for an upright sign (including where at least one method must be used), more than one of those methods may be used.

(7) The same method used to illuminate an upright sign must be used to illuminate an associated plate (and where more than one method is used, all those methods must be used).

(8) The same source of lighting used to illuminate an upright sign may be used to illuminate an associated plate provided it is adequate to do so.

(9) If an upright sign is not illuminated, any associated plate must not be illuminated.

(10) Where retroreflecting material is used on any part of an upright sign or plate, all other parts, other than any parts coloured black, must also be reflectorised.

(11) In paragraph (10) *"part"* means any part which is uniformly coloured and bounded by differently coloured parts.

Illumination – road markings

9.—(1) A road marking may be reflectorised. **B71.10**

(2) Paragraph (1) is subject to provision made elsewhere in these Regulations in relation to particular types of marking.

Height of road markings and size of studs fitted with reflectors, retroreflecting material or a light source

10.—(1) No road marking may project above the surface of the adjacent car- **B71.11**

riageway more than 6 mm at any point except where a provision to that effect is made elsewhere in these Regulations.

(2) A depressible stud must not project more than 25 mm above the surface of the carriageway.

(3) A non-depressible stud must not project more than 20 mm above the surface of the carriageway.

(4) Paragraph (5) applies to a stud which, in accordance with these Regulations, is fitted with reflectors, retroreflecting material, a light source or a combination.

(5) The part of a stud which is visible when the stud is in place must have—

(a) an overall length in the direction of travel of traffic of not less than 35 mm and not more than 250 mm; and

(b) an overall width of not less than 84 mm and not more than 190 mm.

Diagram Colours

B71.12   **11.**—(1) The colours prescribed for signs must conform to British Standard BS EN 12899-1:2007.

(2) Paragraph (1) does not apply—

(a) if alternative provision is made elsewhere in these Regulations in relation to a sign; or

(b) to the extent it is provided that part of a sign may be of any, or any contrasting, colour.

Mutual recognition of standards

B71.13   **12.** Any requirement in these Regulations to comply with a specified British Standard is satisfied by compliance with—

(a) a standard or code of practice of a national standards body or equivalent body of any EEA State,

(b) any international standard recognised for use as a standard or code of practice by any EEA State, or

(c) a technical specification recognised for use as a standard by a public authority of any EEA State,

which requires a level of performance equivalent to that required by the specified British Standard.

***

Transitional and savings provisions

B71.14   **14.**—(1) Paragraph (2) applies to a sign—

(a) where the sign is in place immediately before the coming into force of these Regulations; or

(b) where the sign is referred to in paragraph (4) and is placed within a period of 12 weeks beginning with the day on which these Regulations come into force.

(2) A sign to which this paragraph applies and which is of a size, colour and type prescribed, or treated as prescribed, by the Traffic Signs Regulations 2002 ("the 2002 Regulations") is to be treated as being of a size, colour and type prescribed by these Regulations.

(3) A sign shown by diagram 2919.1 is not to be treated as being of a size, colour and type prescribed by these Regulations on or after 30th January 2022.

(4) The signs referred to in paragraph (1)(b) are those shown by, or including as an element—

(a) diagram 515.2, 530, 532.2, 532.3, 574, 618.2, 618.3, 618.3A, 618.4, 629, 629.1, 629.2, 780A, 780.1A, 780.2A, 826, 826.1, 864.1 or 953.2;

(b) where the arrow symbols are of the maximum dimension permitted by the 2002 Regulations, diagram 868, 868.1, 872.1, 873, 874 or 875; and

(c) where the lower case letters are of the maximum height permitted by the 2002 Regulations, diagram 876,

or any of those diagrams varied in accordance with the 2002 Regulations.

(5) The Zebra, Pelican and Puffin Pedestrian Crossings Regulations 1997 ("the 1997 Regulations") are to be treated as remaining in force in relation to Pelican crossings (within the meaning of those Regulations) established—

(a) before the coming into force of these Regulations; or

(b) within a period of six months beginning with the day on which these Regulations come into force.

(6) In their application to Pelican crossings for the purposes of paragraph (5), the 1997 Regulations are modified in accordance with paragraphs (7) and (8).

(7) The exceptions to the prohibition imposed by regulation 12(1)(c) and (d) of the 1997 Regulations (about proceeding beyond a stop line when a steady amber or red signal is showing) are those at paragraph 5(4) to (6) of Part 1 of Schedule 14 to this Instrument and not those at regulation 12(1)(e) to (ec) of the 1997 Regulations (with the reference in paragraph 5(4) to the prohibition in sub-paragraph (3) treated as being instead a reference to the prohibition in paragraph (c) or (d) in regulation 12(1)).

(8) The exceptions to the prohibition imposed by regulation 20 of the 1997 Regulations (about stopping in a controlled area) in regulation 21(c) to (e) of those Regulations do not apply and instead the exceptions set out in paragraph 4(2)(d) of Part 5 of Schedule 14 to this Instrument apply.

(9) In this regulation, a reference to a diagram number is to that diagram number in the 2002 Regulations.

Provision for review of these Regulations

B71.15   **15.**—(1) The Secretary of State must from time to time—

(a) carry out a review of these Regulations;

(b) set out the conclusions of the review in a report; and

(c) publish the report.

(2) The report must in particular—

(a) set out the objectives intended to be achieved by the regulatory system established by these Regulations;

(b) assess the extent to which those objectives are achieved; and

(c) assess whether those objectives remain appropriate and, if so, the extent to which they could be achieved with a system that imposes less regulation.

(3) The first report under this regulation must be published before the end of the period of five years beginning with the day on which these Regulations come into force.

(4) Reports under this regulation are afterwards to be published at intervals not exceeding five years.

Signed by authority of the Secretary of State

PART 2

THE TRAFFIC SIGNS GENERAL DIRECTIONS 2016

Citation, commencement and extent

B71.16   **1.** *[Omitted.]*

Interpretation

B71.17   **2.**—(1) In these General Directions, *"the Regulations"* means the Traffic Signs Regulations 2016.

(2) Other words and expressions used in these General Directions, which are also used in the Regulations, have the same meaning as in the Regulations.

Application of general directions

B71.18   **3.** The general directions in the final Part of each of Schedules 2 to 15 apply to the signs provided for in that Schedule to the extent indicated in the Schedule.

General provision about upright signs and associated plates and structure warning markings

B71.19   **4.**—(1) A plate or structure warning marking may only be placed in conjunction with an upright sign with which it is associated.

106

(2) An upright sign which has an associated plate or structure warning marking may be placed with or without that associated plate or structure warning marking.

(3) Paragraph (2) does not apply in relation to a particular sign to the extent provision is made elsewhere in these General Directions about the placing of the sign with an associated plate or structure warning marking which contradicts paragraph (2).

General provision about placing of signs on vehicles

5. A sign must not be placed on a vehicle except as expressly authorised by these General Directions. **B71.20**

General provision about the removal of temporary signs

6.—(1) Paragraph (2) applies to a sign placed for conveying to traffic a warning, information, requirement, restriction or prohibition of a temporary nature. **B71.21**

(2) The sign must not remain in place for longer than it is needed.

(3) Paragraph (2) does not apply in relation to a particular sign to the extent provision is made elsewhere in these General Directions about the removal of that sign.

Studs that provide illumination

7.—(1) A stud provided for in the Regulations that incorporates reflectors, retroreflecting material, a light source or any combination may only be placed if it complies with this general direction. **B71.22**

(2) If it incorporates reflectors or retroreflecting material, but no light source, a stud complies with this general direction if it is of a type which meets the applicable requirements and test specifications of the British Standard for retroreflecting studs.

(3) The applicable requirements and test specifications of the British Standard for retroreflecting studs for a type of stud of a description in column 2 of an item in the table are those shown in column 3.

(1)	*(2)*	*(3)*
Item	*Description of stud*	*British Standard requirement or test specification and class*
1	Non depressible road stud	Dimensions : height-class H1 or H2
2	Depressible road stud	Dimensions : height-class H1, H2 or H3

107

(1)	(2)	(3)
Item	Description of stud	British Standard requirement or test specification and class
3	Permanent road stud	Dimensions : maximum horizontal dimension exposed to traffic: HD1
4	Temporary road stud	Dimensions : minimum horizontal dimension exposed to traffic: HDT1
5	Permanent road stud	Night-time visibility : photometric requirements - class PRP1
6	Temporary road stud	Night-time visibility : photometric requirements - class PRT1
7	Temporary road stud	Daytime visibility : colour of body of stud — class DCR1 fluorescent green-yellow — class DV1
8	Any stud	Colorimetric requirements-class NCR1 for white, amber, red or green retroreflectors only
9	Any stud	Primary assessment-class S1
10	Any stud	Night-time visibility assessment-class R1, R2 or R3

(4) The appropriate national authority may approve the placing of a type of stud on a road for the purpose of testing whether that type complies with the applicable requirements and test specifications of the British Standard for retroreflecting studs mentioned in paragraph (3).

(5) A stud which incorporates a light source (whether or not it also incorporates reflectors or retroreflecting material) complies with this general direction if it is of a type which has been approved for use on roads by the appropriate national authority.

(6) Approval under paragraph (4) or (5) must be given by a notice in writing to the supplier of the stud.

(7) The notice may provide that approval is for a specified time period only.

(8) A time period may be varied by a subsequent notice and a subsequent notice may provide for a time period where one has not previously been given.

(9) All studs ceasing to be of an approved type by reason of the expiry of a time period must be removed before the expiry of that period.

(10) In this general direction *"national authority"*—

    (a) in relation to roads in England and Wales, means the Secretary of State; and

    (b) in relation to roads in Scotland, means the Scottish Ministers.

(11) An approval having effect immediately before the coming into force of these Regulations that applies in relation to roads in Scotland is to be treated as having been given by the Scottish Ministers in relation to those roads.

Mounting of upright signs

8.—(1) Where an upright sign is mounted on a post or other support specially **B71.23**
provided for the purpose, the part of the post or support above the ground must
be—

    (a) a single colour; or

    (b) the natural colour of the post or support,

but paragraphs (2), (3) and (5) provide for exceptions.

(2) Where the post or support is not likely to be readily visible to pedestrians, cyclists or equestrians, a yellow or white band not less than 140 mm nor more than 160 mm deep may be provided on the post with the lower edge of the band being not less than 1500 mm nor more than 1700 mm above ground level.

(3) Where the support provided for a portable upright sign comprises several components, the components need not all be of the same colour provided that each is of a single colour or the natural colour of the component.

(4) Paragraphs (1) to (3) do not apply to the mounting of a particular upright sign to the extent provision is made elsewhere in these General Directions about the post or other support for that sign.

(5) An identification code for maintenance purposes may be indicated, in characters not exceeding 25 mm in height, on a post or support on which an upright sign is mounted.

The backs of, and backing boards for, upright signs

9.—(1) Paragraph (2) applies to— **B71.24**

    (a) the back of an upright sign;

    (b) the back of any backing board; and

    (c) any other fitting provided for the assembly of a sign (including any container enclosing apparatus for the illumination of a sign).

(2) The back or other fitting must be grey, black or in a non-reflective metallic finish.

(3) Paragraphs (4) and (5) are exceptions to paragraph (2).

(4) Information about sites for placing, and the ownership of, the sign, and an identification code for maintenance purposes, may be indicated on the back of the sign in characters not exceeding—

    (a) 25 mm in height, where they are shown in a contrasting colour; or

    (b) 50 mm in height, where they are embossed in the same colour.

(5) Information about the manufacture of the sign required in order to comply with—

(a) British Standard BS EN 12899-1:2007; or

(b) a corresponding EEA Standard,

occupying an area not exceeding 30 square centimetres, may be indicated on the back of the sign in characters not exceeding 5 mm in height.

(6) The front of any backing board for an upright sign must be coloured either grey or yellow.

(7) If the front of the backing board is coloured yellow it may be—

(a) reflectorised;

(b) fluorescent; or

(c) both reflectorised and fluorescent.

(8) Where the front of the backing board is coloured yellow, the board must be rectangular in shape.

(9) This general direction does not apply to the extent provision is made elsewhere in these General Directions about the backs of, and backing boards for, particular upright signs.

Mutual recognition of standards

B71.25   **10.** Any requirement in these General Directions to comply with a specified British Standard is satisfied by compliance with—

(a) a standard or code of practice of a national standards body or equivalent body of any EEA State,

(b) any international standard recognised for use as a standard or code of practice by any EEA State, or

(c) a technical specification recognised for use as a standard by a public authority of any EEA State,

which requires a level of performance equivalent to that required by the British Standard specified.

Special directions

B71.26   **11.** Nothing in these General Directions limits the power of the Secretary of State, the Scottish Ministers or the Welsh Ministers, by special direction under section 65(2) of the 1984 Act, to dispense with, add to or modify any of the requirements of these General Directions in their application to any particular case.

***

Saving

B71.27   **13.**—(1) This general direction applies to a sign that is in place immediately before the coming into force of these General Directions which does not, but for this general direction, comply with these General Directions.

(2) For so long as the way in which it is placed would have conformed with the Pelican and Puffin Pedestrian Crossings General Directions 1997 or the Traffic Signs General Directions 2002, it is to be treated as having been placed in conformity with these General Directions.

Provision for review of these General Directions

14.—(1) The Secretary of State must from time to time—   **B71.28**
    (a) carry out a review of these General Directions;
    (b) set out the conclusions of the review in a report; and
    (c) publish the report.

(2) The report must in particular—
    (a) set out the objectives intended to be achieved by the regulatory system established by these General Directions;
    (b) assess the extent to which those objectives are achieved; and
    (c) assess whether those objectives remain appropriate and, if so, the extent to which they could be achieved with a system that imposes less regulation.

(3) The first report under this regulation must be published before the end of the period of five years beginning with the day on which these General Directions come into force.

(4) Reports under this general direction are afterwards to be published at intervals not exceeding five years.

Signed by authority of the Secretary of State

SCHEDULE 1

DEFINITIONS

B71.29

(1)	(2)
Term	*Meaning*
"abnormal transport unit"	(a) a motor vehicle or a vehicle combination— (i) the overall length of which, inclusive of the load (if any) on the vehicle or the combination, exceeds 61 feet 6 inches (18.75 metres); (ii) the overall width of which, inclusive of the load (if any) on the vehicle or the combination, exceeds 9 feet 6 inches (2.9 metres); or (iii) the maximum gross weight of which exceeds 44 tonnes; or (b) a motor vehicle, or a vehicle combination, which is incapable of proceeding, or is unlikely to proceed, over a level crossing at a speed exceeding 5 mph

Legislation

(1)	(2)
Term	*Meaning*
"actively managed hard shoulder"	a hard shoulder along which, by virtue of regulations under section 17(2) and (3) of the 1984 Act, vehicular traffic may be driven at times for the time being indicated by signs in accordance with those regulations
"administrative area"	(a) United Kingdom; (b) England; (c) Scotland; (d) Wales; (e) a county or district in England for the purposes of the Local Government Act 1972; (f) a county or county borough in Wales for the purposes of the Local Government Act 1972; (g) a local government area for the purposes of the Local Government etc. (Scotland) Act 1994; (h) a London Borough; (i) Greater London; (j) the City of London; (k) the Isles of Scilly
"all-purpose road"	a road that is not a motorway
"amber light beacon"	a beacon which shows an intermittent amber light and which complies with the beacon requirements
"articulated vehicle"	a motor vehicle with a trailer so attached to it as to be partially superimposed upon it
"backing board"	includes any background (except a wall to which a sign is fixed) against which a sign is displayed
"beacon requirements"	the requirements applying to beacons and which are specified in Part 10 of Schedule 13
"blood and blood components"	have the same meaning as in regulation 1(3) of the Blood Safety and Quality Regulations 2005
"blood service purposes"	the collection or distribution of blood or blood components by NHS Blood and Transplant, the Scottish National Blood Transfusion Service, the Welsh Blood Service or the Northern Ireland Blood Transfusion Service
"blue light beacon"	a beacon showing an intermittent blue light which complies with the beacon requirements
"breakdown vehicle"	has the same meaning as in regulation 3(2) of the Road Vehicle Lighting Regulations 1989
"British Standard for retroreflecting studs"	British Standard BS EN 1463-1: 2009 on retro reflecting road studs when read with British Standard BS EN 1463-2: 2000 on road test performance for retroreflecting road studs
"bus"	unless the context requires otherwise— (a) a motor vehicle constructed or adapted to carry more than 8 passengers (exclusive of the driver); or (b) a local bus

(1)	(2)
Term	Meaning
"bus lane"	a traffic lane reserved for— (a) buses; and (b) where indicted on a sign, authorised vehicles, pedal cycles, solo motor cycles or taxis
"carriageway"	(a) in relation to a highway in England or Wales, or a road in Scotland, a way constituting or comprised in the highway or road being a way over which the public has a right of way for the passage of vehicles or class of vehicles, and (b) in relation to any other road in England or Wales to which the public has access, that part of the road to which vehicles have access, but does not include in either case any central reservation
"central reservation"	(a) any land between the carriageways of a road comprising two carriageways; or (b) any permanent work (other than a traffic island) in the carriageway of a road, which separates the carriageway or, as the case may be, the part of the carriageway, which is to be used by traffic moving in one direction from the carriageway or part of the carriageway which is to be used (whether at all times or at particular times only) by traffic moving in the other direction
"ceremonial area"	(a) in relation to England, an area that is to be regarded as a county for the purposes of the Lieutenancies Act 1997 ("the 1997 Act") by virtue of paragraph 3 of Schedule 1 to that Act; (b) in relation to Wales, a preserved county within the meaning of paragraph 6 of Schedule 1 to the 1997 Act; (c) in relation to Scotland, an area for the purposes of the 1997 Act within the meaning of paragraph 7 of Schedule 1 to that Act
"circular sign"	an upright sign which is of a circular shape
"civil emergency"	an emergency within the meaning of section 1 of the Civil Contingencies Act 2004 or terrorism within the meaning of section 1 of the Terrorism Act 2000
"civil emergency warning or information"	a warning or information about a civil emergency or the prospect of a civil emergency
"congestion charging zone"	an area in which the roads are designated for the purposes of a scheme for imposing charges in respect of the keeping or use of motor vehicles on roads

(1)	*(2)*
Term	*Meaning*
"contraflow"	a carriageway, or part of a carriageway, of a road where— (a) traffic is authorised to proceed in the opposite direction to the usual direction of traffic on that part; or (b) a specified class of traffic is authorised to proceed in the opposite direction to other traffic on that carriageway
"controlled parking zone"	either— (a) an area— (i) in which every part of every road is subject to a prohibition indicated by single or double yellow lines or single or double yellow kerb markings (except where parking spaces have been provided, where entrance to or exit from the road is made, where there is a prohibition or restriction on waiting, stopping, loading or unloading indicated by a different sign or where there is a crossing) whether or not an upright sign to indicate the same prohibition is placed in conjunction with the line or kerb marking; and (ii) into which each entrance for vehicular traffic has been indicated by the sign provided for at item 1 or 3 of the sign table in Part 3 of Schedule 5; or (b) an area— (i) in which at least one sign provided for at item 3 of the sign table in Part 3 of Schedule 4 has been placed on each side of every road; and (ii) in which each entrance for vehicular traffic has been indicated by a sign provided for at item 4 of the sign table in Part 3 of Schedule 5
"corresponding EEA standard"	a standard, code of practice or technical specification of a kind referred to in regulation 12 which requires a level of performance equivalent to that required by a British Standard
"cycle lane"	part of a carriageway of a road reserved for pedal cycles which is separated from the rest of the carriageway— (a) if it may not be used by vehicles other than pedal cycles, by the marking provided for at item 7 of the sign table in Part 6 of Schedule 9; (b) if it may be used by vehicles other than pedal cycles when clear of pedal cycles, by the marking provided for at item 2 or 3 of the sign table in Part 4 of Schedule 11
"cycle track"	(a) in relation to England and Wales, has the same meaning as in section 329(1) of the Highways Act 1980; (b) in relation to Scotland, has the same meaning as in section 151(2)(b) of the Roads (Scotland) Act 1984

(1)	(2)
Term	Meaning
"depressible stud"	a stud fitted in such a way that the height by which it, or part of it, projects above the surface of the adjacent carriageway is reduced when pressure is applied from above
"designated lane"	a traffic lane reserved, by an order under section 1, 6, 9, 14, 16A or 19 of the 1984 Act (traffic regulation orders and orders similar to traffic regulation orders), for use by such class of vehicular traffic as is, by the order, specified for the purpose of that reservation
"disabled badge holder symbol"	refers to this symbol:
"double red lines"	the road marking provided for at item 11 of the sign table in Part 4 of Schedule 7
"double yellow kerb marking"	the road marking provided for at item 3 of the sign table in Part 4 of Schedule 7
"double yellow lines"	the road marking provided for at item 1 of the sign table in Part 4 of Schedule 7
"driver"	(a) in relation to a vehicle which is a motor cycle or pedal cycle, the person riding the vehicle who is, or is purporting to be, in control of it; and (b) in relation to an abnormal transport unit— (i) where that unit is a single motor vehicle the driver of that vehicle; or (ii) where that unit is a vehicle combination, the driver of the only or the foremost motor vehicle forming part of that combination
"dual carriageway road"	a road which comprises a central reservation and "all-purpose dual carriageway road" means a dual carriageway road which is not a motorway
"emergency vehicle"	has the same meaning as in regulation 3(2) of the Road Vehicle Lighting Regulations 1989
"equestrian crossing"	a place on the carriageway of a road— (a) at which provision is made for equestrian traffic to cross the carriageway; and (b) the presence of which is indicated by a combination of— (i) the traffic light signals provided for at item 1, 3 or 4 of the sign table in Part 2 of Schedule 14; (ii) the signals provided for at— (aa) items 15 and 16 of that table; or (bb) the signal provided for at item 17 (whether or not placed with the signal provided for at item 18); and (iii) the road marking provided for at item 55 or 56
"excursion or tour"	has the meaning given in section 137(1) of the Transport Act 1985

Legislation

(1)	(2)
Term	Meaning
"fire and rescue authority"	is to be construed in accordance with section 1 of the Fire and Rescue Services Act 2004
"fluorescent greenyellow"	has the same meaning as in the British Standard for retroreflecting studs
"General Directions"	the Traffic Signs General Directions 2016
"give way sign"	the upright sign provided for at item 2 in the Part 2 sign table in Schedule 9
"goods vehicle"	a motor vehicle or trailer constructed or adapted for use for the carriage or haulage of goods or burden of any description (and a reference in a diagram to *"t"* is to the maximum gross weight in tonnes)
"hard shoulder"	in relation to a motorway in England and Wales, has the meaning given by regulation 3(1)(e) of the Motorways Traffic (England and Wales) Regulations 1982 and, in relation to a motorway in Scotland, regulation 2(1) of the Motorways Traffic (Scotland) Regulations 1995
"historic county area"	an area that at the time of the placing of the sign in question is not, but was, a county
"hours of darkness"	the time between half an hour after sunset and half an hour before sunrise
"junction"	a road junction
"layout or character"	in relation to a road, means the layout or character of the road itself and does not include the layout or character of any land or premises adjacent to the road
"leisure facility"	(a) those facilities of a description in column 2 of— (i) items 4 to 12 in Part 14 of Schedule 12; (ii) items 4, 12, 18, 34 to 38, 43, 44, 60, 63, 64 and 67 of Part 15 of Schedule 12; (iii) item 4 of Part 16 of Schedule 12; (iv) item 4 of Part 18 of Schedule 12; (b) a tourist hostel
"level crossing"	a place where a road is crossed by a railway or tramway on a reserved track on the same level
"local"	when shown on a bus symbol, indicates that the road or the traffic lane on or near which the sign has been placed must be used only by local buses.
"local bus"	a public service vehicle used for the provision of a local service not being an excursion or tour
"local service"	has the meaning given in section 2 of the Transport Act 1985
"major road"	the road at a junction into which there emerges vehicular traffic from a minor road
"matrix sign"	a light signal for conveying information or a warning, requirement, restriction, prohibition or speed limit to traffic on a motorway, or an allpurpose dual carriageway road

(1)	(2)
Term	Meaning
"*maximum gross weight*"	(a) in the case of a motor vehicle not drawing a trailer or in the case of a trailer, its maximum laden weight; (b) in the case of an articulated vehicle, its maximum laden weight (if it has one) and otherwise the aggregate maximum laden weight of all the individual vehicles forming part of that articulated vehicle; (c) in the case of a motor vehicle (other than an articulated vehicle) drawing one or more trailers, the aggregate maximum laden weight of the motor vehicle and the trailer or trailers drawn by it
"*maximum laden weight*"	in relation to a vehicle (including a vehicle which is a trailer) means— (a) in the case of a vehicle as respects which a gross weight not to be exceeded in Great Britain is specified in construction and use requirements (as defined by section 41(7) of the Road Traffic Act 1988), the weight so specified; (b) in the case of a vehicle as respects which no such weight is so specified, the weight which the vehicle is designed or adapted not to exceed when in normal use and travelling on a road laden;
"*maximum speed limit sign*"	the sign provided for at item 1 of the sign table in Part 2 of Schedule 10
"*method of illumination*"	is a reference to illumination by internal or external lighting or reflectorisation
"*minor road*"	a road on which, at its junction with another road, there is placed the sign at item 1 or 2 of the sign table in Part 2 of Schedule 9 or the road marking at item 3 of the sign table in Part 6 of that Schedule
"*minor route*"	a road which, under the system for assigning identification numbers to roads administered by the Secretary of State, Scottish Ministers or Welsh Ministers, has not been assigned a number prefixed by A, B or M
"*mobile road works*"	road works carried out by or from a vehicle or vehicles which move slowly along the road or which stop briefly from time to time along that road
"*motorway*"	a special road which— (a) in England and Wales (except if otherwise provided by or under regulations made under, or having effect as if made under, section 17 of the 1984 Act), can be used by traffic only of Class I or Class II as specified in Schedule 4 to the Highways Act 1980; (b) in Scotland, can be used by traffic only of Class I or Class II as specified in Schedule 3 to the Roads (Scotland) Act 1984
"*mph*"	miles per hour

(1)	(2)
Term	*Meaning*
"national promoter of tourism"	(a) in relation to England, the British Tourist Authority; (b) in relation to Scotland, VisitScotland; and (c) in relation to Wales, Welsh Ministers
"national speed limit"	any prohibition imposed on a road by the 70 miles per hour, 60 miles per hour and 50 miles per hour (Temporary Speed Limit) Order 1977 or by regulation 3 of the Motorways Traffic (Speed Limits) Regulations 1974
"NHS ambulance service"	(a) an NHS trust or NHS foundation trust established under the National Health Service Act 2006 which has a function of providing ambulance services; (b) an NHS trust established under the National Health Service (Wales) Act 2006 which has a function of providing ambulance services; (c) the Scottish Ambulance Service Board
"non-primary route"	a route, not being a primary route or a motorway or part of a primary route or of a motorway
"panel"	a rectangular or square part of a sign which is distinguishable from the other part or parts of the sign by being of a contrasting colour or having a border of a contrasting colour

"Parallel controlled area"	a length of carriageway—
	(a) which—
	  (i) is adjacent to a Parallel crossing; and
	  (ii) in the manner shown in the diagram at item 53 of the sign table in Part 2 of Schedule 14, has a zig-zag line, of the type provided for at that item, marked along each of its edges (with or without zig-zag lines also marked down its centre) and give way markings, of the type provided for at item 54 of that table, marked parallel to the crossing; and
	(b) in or near which no other signs or markings have been placed except ones—
	  (i) comprised in the combination of signs and markings indicating the presence of the facility for crossing; or
	  (ii) provided for at item—
	    (aa) 3, 7, 8 or 10 in the sign table in Part 2 of Schedule 3;
	    (bb) 2 or 73 in the sign table in Part 2 of Schedule 11; or
	    (cc) 18, 28 or 33 in the sign table in Part 4 of Schedule 11

(1)	(2)
Term	Meaning

"Parallel crossing"	a place on the carriageway—
	(a) where provision is made for pedestrians and cyclists to cross the carriageway;
	(b) the presence of which is indicated by—
	  (i) a yellow globe of the type provided for at item 27 of the sign table in Part 2 of Schedule 14 at each end of the crossing (except that globes need not be present at a crossing that only crosses a cycle track);
	  (ii) in respect of the part of the crossing for pedestrians, the black and white stripes shown in the diagram at item 53 and in respect of which provision is made at paragraph 18 of Part 1 of that Schedule (including provision for the black stripes to be a different colour); and
	  (iii) in respect of the part of the crossing for cyclists, the markings provided for at item 57 together with, where used, the cycle symbols shown in the diagram at item 53 of that sign table; and
	(c) the limits of which are indicated—
	  (i) in so far as they relate to the part for pedestrians, the stripes; and
	  (ii) in so far as they relate to the part for cyclists, the marking at item 57

"parking place identifier"	any symbol, logo, letter, numeral or name (or combination) of any size in a colour that contrasts with the background on which they are placed, whether or not placed on a patch which may be of any colour, which indicates or identifies an area or location in which restrictions on the parking of vehicles apply by reference to a particular parking place or group of parking places
"pedal cycle"	a unicycle, bicycle, tricycle or cycle having four or more wheels, not being in any case mechanically propelled unless it is an electrically assisted pedal cycle that is not treated as a motor vehicle for the purposes of the 1984 Act
"pedestrian zone"	an area— (a) which has been laid out to improve amenity for pedestrians; and (b) to which the entry of vehicles is prohibited or restricted
"pedestrian and cycle zone"	an area— (a) which has been laid out to improve amenity for pedestrians and cyclists; and (b) to which the entry of vehicles, except pedal cycles, is prohibited or restricted
"permit identifier"	any upper case letter or letters, with or without a number, whether or not placed on a patch which may be of any colour, where the letter and, as the case may be, number are of any size, in a colour that contrasts with the background on which they are placed and indicate a type of permit

(1)	*(2)*
Term	*Meaning*
"permit parking area"	an area— (a) into which each entrance for vehicular traffic has been indicated by the sign provided for at item 5 of the sign table in Part 3 of Schedule 5; and (b) where any parking place within that area reserved for the use of the permit holders as indicated on that sign is not shown by markings on the road (whether or not an upright sign is placed next to, or near, such a parking place to indicate that only the permit holders in question may use the place)
"plate"	a sign which may or must (as indicated in the General Directions) be used to supplement or qualify the message conveyed by an upright sign. And an *"associated plate"* refers to a plate which supplements or qualifies a particular upright sign
"police vehicle"	a vehicle being used for police purposes or operating under the instructions of a chief officer of police
"portable signal controlled pedestrian facility"	a place on the carriageway— (a) which is not a section 25 crossing; (b) where temporary provision is made for pedestrians to cross the carriageway; (c) the presence of which is indicated by the signs provided for in the sign table in Part 2 of Schedule 14 at item 2, item 60 and — (i) item 9 (with or without item 10) and either item 11 or 12; or (ii) item 13; and (d) the presence of which may in addition be indicated by— (i) either or both of the road markings provided for at item 46 (stop line) and 55 (crossing marking) of the table; and (ii) where— (aa) all streams of vehicular traffic are stopped only for the purpose of enabling pedestrians to cross the carriageway; and (bb) both the stop line and crossing markings provided for at items 46 and 55 respectively are also placed, the road marking provided for at item 51 of the table
"primary route"	a route, not being a route comprising any part of a motorway, in relation to which a determination has been made that it provides the most satisfactory route for through traffic between places of traffic importance under the administrative system for so determining that is the responsibility of the Secretary of State, Scottish Ministers or Welsh Ministers in England, Scotland and Wales respectively

(1)	(2)
Term	Meaning
"principal road"	(a) in England and Wales, a road classified as a principal road in accordance with section 12 of the Highways Act 1980 (whether as falling within subsection (1) or classified under subsection (3)); (b) in Scotland, a road classified as a principal road in accordance with section 11(1) of the Roads (Scotland) Act 1984
"Puffin controlled area"	a length of carriageway— (a) which is adjacent to a Puffin crossing, has a zig-zag line marked along each of its edges (with or without zig-zag lines also marked down its centre) and is shown by the markings in the diagram at item 51 of the sign table in Part 2 of Schedule 14 and stop line markings, of the type provided for at item 46 or 49 of that table, marked parallel to the crossing; and (b) in or near which no other signs or markings have been placed except ones— (i) comprised in the combination of signs and markings indicating the presence of the facility for crossing; or (ii) provided for at item— (aa) 3, 7, 8 or 10 in the sign table in Part 2 of Schedule 3; (bb) 2 or 73 in the sign table in Part 2 of Schedule 11; or (cc) 18, 28 or 33 in the sign table in Part 4 of Schedule 11
"Puffin crossing"	a section 25 crossing— (a) where provision is made for pedestrians to cross the carriageway; and (b) the presence of which is indicated by a combination of— (i) the traffic light signals provided for at item 1, 3 or 4 of the sign table in Part 2 of Schedule 14; (ii) the nearside light signals provided for at item 13 (whether or not used with the supplementary nearside signals provided for at item 14) of that table; and (iii) the crossing marking provided for at item 55 of that table
"red route"	a road in respect of which the prohibition indicated by single or double red lines has been imposed by an order or notice under the 1984 Act (subject to such exceptions as are provided for by such an order or notice). This definition does not apply when *"red route"* is used in the phrase *"red route clearway"*

Legislation

(1)	(2)
Term	*Meaning*
"red route clearway"	a road in respect of which the prohibition indicated by the sign provided for at item 8 of the sign table in Part 2 of Schedule 7 has been imposed by an order or notice under the 1984 Act (subject to such exceptions as are provided for by such an order or notice)
"reflectorised"	illuminated by the use of retroreflecting material (and *"reflectorisation"* is to be construed accordingly)
"retroreflecting material"	material which reflects a ray of light back towards the source of that light
"refuge for pedestrians"	a part of a road to which vehicles do not have access and on which pedestrians may wait after crossing one part of the carriageway and before crossing the other
"restricted parking zone"	an area— (a) into which each entrance for vehicular traffic has been indicated by a sign which includes the symbol and legend at item 2 of the sign table in Part 3 of Schedule 5; and (b) in which none of the road markings at items 1 to 4 of the sign table in Part 4 of Schedule 7 has been placed
"road maintenance vehicle"	a vehicle which is specially designed or adapted for use on a road by or on behalf of a traffic authority for the purposes of road maintenance
"road marking"	a sign consisting of a line, mark or legend on a road
"road works"	works for the improvement, alteration or maintenance of a road and includes— (a) in relation to England and Wales, street works as defined by section 48(3) of the New Roads and Street Works Act 1991; (b) in relation to Scotland, road works as defined by section 107(3) of that Act
" Schedule [x] General Direction"	where [x] is replaced by a number, is a reference to a general direction that, pursuant to general direction 3 in Part 2 of this Instrument, is contained in the Schedule bearing that number
"school crossing patrol sign"	a sign exhibited by a school crossing patrol for the purpose of stopping a vehicle in accordance with section 28(1) of the 1984 Act and provided for at item 24 of the sign table in Part 2 of Schedule 14
"school crossing place"	a place in a road where children cross or seek to cross that road on their way to or from school or on their way from one part of a school to another
" section 25 crossing"	a Puffin crossing or a Zebra crossing
" section 25 crossing controlled area"	a Puffin-controlled area or a Zebra-controlled area
"sign"	a traffic sign or a school crossing patrol sign

(1)	(2)
Term	*Meaning*
"sign table"	a table in Schedules 2 to 15 that is headed "Sign table" (followed by the Schedule and Part in which the table appears)
"signal-controlled crossing facility"	an equestrian crossing, a signal-controlled pedestrian facility or a Toucan crossing
"signal-controlled crossing facility controlled area"	a length of carriageway— (a) which is adjacent to a signal-controlled crossing facility and has a zig-zag line marked along each of its edges (with or without zig-zag lines also marked down its centre) and is shown by the markings in the diagram at item 51 of the sign table in Part 2 of Schedule 14 and stop line markings, of the type provided for at item 46 or 49 of that table, marked parallel to the crossing; and (b) in or near which no other signs or markings have been placed except ones— (i) comprised in the combination of signs and markings indicating the presence of the facility for crossing; or (ii) provided for at item— (aa) 3, 7, 8 or 10 in the sign table in Part 2 of Schedule 3; (bb) 2 or 73 in the sign table in Part 2 of Schedule 11; or (cc) 18, 28 or 33 in the sign table in Part 4 of Schedule 11
"signal-controlled pedestrian facility"	a place on the carriageway of a road— (a) which is not a section 25 crossing; (b) where provision is made for pedestrians to cross the carriageway; and (c) the presence of which is indicated by a combination of— (i) the traffic light signals provided for at item 1, 3 or 4 of the sign table in Part 2 of Schedule 14; (ii) the sign provided for at— (aa) item 9 (with or without item 10) and either item 11 or 12 of the sign table in Part 2 of Schedule 14; or (bb) item 13 of the table (whether or not placed with the signal provided for at item 14); and (iii) the road marking provided for at item 55 or 56 of the table
"single red line"	the road marking provided for at item 12 of the sign table in Part 4 of Schedule 7
"single yellow kerb marking"	the road marking provided for at item 4 of the sign table in Part 4 of Schedule 7
"single yellow line"	the road marking provided for at item 2 of the sign table in Part 4 of Schedule 7

(1)	(2)
Term	Meaning
"solo motor cycle"	a motor cycle without a side car
"special forces purposes"	the use of a vehicle for naval, military or air force purposes where— (a) the person driving the vehicle is a member of a unit of the armed forces of the Crown the maintenance of whose capabilities is the responsibility of the Director of Special Forces or which is for the time being subject to the operational command of that Director; and (b) the vehicle is being driven— (i) in response, or for practice in responding to, a national security emergency by a person who has been trained in driving vehicles at high speeds; or (ii) for the purpose of training a person in driving vehicles at high speeds
"speed limit"	a maximum or minimum limit of speed on the driving of vehicles on a road— (a) imposed by an order under section 14 of the 1984 Act (temporary prohibition or restriction of traffic on roads); (b) imposed by an order under section 16A of the 1984 Act (special events); (c) imposed by regulations under section 17 of the 1984 Act (traffic regulation on special roads); (d) arising by virtue of the road being restricted for the purposes of section 81 of the 1984 Act (general speed limit for restricted roads); (e) imposed by an order under section 84 of the 1984 Act (speed limits on roads other than restricted roads); (f) imposed by an order under section 88 of the 1984 Act (temporary speed limits); or (g) imposed by or under a local Act, and *"maximum speed limit"* and *"minimum speed limit"* are to be construed accordingly
"stop line"	has the meaning given in paragraph 30 of Part 1 of Schedule 14
"stop sign"	the upright sign provided for at item 1 in the Part 2 sign table in Schedule 9
"the stopping prohibited symbol"	refers to this symbol:
"stroke width"	25% of the x-height
"structure warning marking"	the markings provided for at items 3 and 4 of the sign table in Part 5 of Schedule 2 which may be used to supplement a triangular or circular sign and in the phrase *"associated structure warning marking"*, *"associated"* refers to the marking in question being supplementary to a particular triangular or circular sign

(1)	(2)
Term	Meaning
"stud"	a prefabricated device fixed or embedded in the carriageway of a road
"system of streetlighting"	the presence on a road of at least three lamps, lit by electricity, provided for the purposes of illuminating the road, and placed no more than— (a) 183 metres apart in England and Wales, or (b) 185 metres apart in Scotland
"taxi"	(a) in England and Wales, a vehicle licensed under— (i) section 37 of the Town Police Clauses Act 1847; or (ii) section 6 of the Metropolitan Public Carriage Act 1869; or under any similar enactment; (b) in Scotland, a taxi licensed under section 10 of the Civic Government (Scotland) Act 1982
"taxi rank"	an area of carriageway reserved for use by taxis waiting to pick up passengers
"temporary hazard warning"	a warning about, or information on how to avoid, any temporary hazards caused by— (a) works being executed on or near a road; (b) adverse weather conditions or other natural causes; (c) the failure of street-lighting or malfunction of, or damage to, any other apparatus, equipment or facility used in connection with the road or anything situated on or near or under it; or (d) damage to the road itself
"temporary information"	(a) information about— (i) the time, date or location of road works; (ii) the expected delay that road works may cause; (iii) convenient routes to be followed on the occasion of a sporting event, an exhibition or any other public gathering which is likely to attract a large volume of traffic; (iv) diversions or alternative routes; (v) check points at which drivers of goods vehicles or public service vehicles may be required to stop; (vi) the availability of new routes or destinations; or (vii) changes in route numbers; (b) information for drivers of wide loads about action to be taken in respect of road works ahead; or (c) requests by the police for information in connection with road traffic accidents
"temporary statutory provision"	(a) a provision having effect under section 9 or section 14 of the 1984 Act or under a provision referred to in section 66 of that Act; (b) a prohibition, restriction or requirement indicated by a sign placed pursuant to section 67 of the 1984 Act; or (c) a provision having effect under section 62 of the Roads (Scotland) Act 1984

Legislation

(1)	(2)
Term	*Meaning*
"terminal sign"	a sign placed to indicate the point at which a requirement, restriction or prohibition begins or ends

"Toucan crossing"	a place on the carriageway of a road—
	  (a) where provision is made for both pedestrians and pedal cyclists to cross the carriageway; and
	  (b) the presence of which is indicated by a combination of—
	    (i) the traffic light signals provided for at item 1, 3 or 4 of the sign table in Part 2 of Schedule 14;
	    (ii)
	      (aa) the signals provided for at item 19 (with or without item 10) and either item 12 or 20 of the sign table in Part 2 of Schedule 14; or
	      (bb) the signal provided for at item 21 of that table (whether or not placed with the signal provided for at item 22 of the table); and
	    (iii) the road marking provided for at item 55 or 56 of the table

"tourist destination"	(a) a Tourist Information Centre or Point;
	(b) a permanently established attraction or facility (other than a leisure facility) which—
	  (i) attracts or is used by visitors to an area;
	  (ii) is open to the public without prior booking during its normal opening hours; and
	  (iii) is recognised as a tourist attraction or facility by the appropriate national promoter of tourism;
	(c) a village, town or city that is of particular interest to tourists;
	(d) a route that is of particular interest to tourists

"Tourist Information Centre"	a staffed information service centre recognised and supported by the appropriate national promoter of tourism
"Tourist Information Point"	a display of tourist information approved by the appropriate national promoter of tourism or another person or body responsible for promoting tourism for a particular village, town or other area of England, Wales or Scotland
"traffic lane"	a part of the carriageway intended for use by vehicles travelling in a particular direction or reserved for use by vehicles of a particular type and separated from other parts of the carriageway by road markings
"traffic light signals"	the light signals provided for at items 1 to 4 of the sign table in Part 2 of Schedule 14
"traffic officer"	has the meaning given in section 100(5) of the 1984 Act
"tramcar"	has the meaning given in section 141A(4) of the 1984 Act
"triangular sign"	an upright sign which is of a triangular shape
"trolley vehicle"	has the meaning given in section 141A(4) of the 1984 Act

(1)	(2)
Term	Meaning
"trunk road"	has the meaning given— (a) as respects England and Wales, in section 329(1) of the Highways Act 1980; (b) as respects Scotland, in section 151(1) of the Roads (Scotland) Act 1984;
"tunnel restriction code"	any of the codes specified in Chapter 1.9 of Part 1 of Annex A to the European Agreement concerning the International Carriage of Dangerous Goods by Road (ADR) as applicable from 1st January 2015
"upright sign"	a traffic sign other than a plate, a structure warning marking, a road marking or light signals
"variable message sign"	a device which complies with the requirements of Part 1 of Schedule 16 and is capable of displaying, at different times, two or more of the following— (a) a sign provided for in Schedule 2 to 13 or 15; (b) a legend provided for in Schedule 16; and (c) a blank grey or a blank black face.
"vehicle combination"	a combination of vehicles made up of one or more motor vehicles and one or more trailers all of which are linked together when travelling
"with-flow"	indicates that the bus or cycle lane in question is for the use of traffic of a type permitted to use that lane proceeding in the same direction as general traffic in an adjoining traffic lane
"x-height"	the height of the lower case "x" in Parts 1 and 2 of Schedule 17
"Zebra controlled area"	a length of carriageway— (a) which— (i) is adjacent to a Zebra crossing; and (ii) in the manner shown in the diagram at item 52 of the sign table in Part 2 of Schedule 14, has a zig-zag line, of the type provided for at that item, marked along each of its edges (with or without zig-zag lines also marked down its centre) and give way markings, of the type provided for at item 54 of that table, marked parallel to the crossing; and (b) in or near which no other signs or markings have been placed except ones— (i) comprised in the combination of signs and markings indicating the presence of the facility for crossing; or (ii) provided for at item— (aa) 3, 7, 8 or 10 in the sign table in Part 2 of Schedule 3; (bb) 2 or 73 in the sign table in Part 2 of Schedule 11; or (cc) 18, 28 or 33 in the sign table in Part 4 of Schedule 11

(1)	*(2)*
Term	*Meaning*
"Zebra crossing"	a place on the carriageway— (a) where provision is made for pedestrians to cross the carriageway; (b) the presence of which is indicated by— (i) a yellow globe of the type provided for at item 27 of the sign table in Part 2 of Schedule 14 at each end of the crossing (except that globes need not be present at a crossing that only crosses a cycle track); (ii) the black and white stripes shown in the diagram at item 52 of that table and in respect of which provision is made at paragraph 18 of Part 1 of that Schedule (including provision for the black stripes to be a different colour); and (iii) where used, the marking provided for at item 55 of that table; and (c) the limits of which are indicated by the stripes except that, where used, the limit is indicated by the marking at item 55
"zone identifier"	any symbol, logo, letter, numeral or name (or combination) of any size in a colour that contrasts with the background on which they are placed, whether or not placed on a patch which may be of any colour, which indicates or identifies an area or location in which restrictions on the parking of vehicles apply by reference to that area or location

SCHEDULES 2–19

[Omitted]

Index

This index has been prepared using Sweet and Maxwell's Legal Taxonomy. Main index entries conform to keywords provided by the Legal Taxonomy except where references to specific documents or non-standard terms (denoted by quotation marks) have been included. These keywords provide a means of identifying similar concepts in other Sweet & Maxwell publications and online services to which keywords from the Legal Taxonomy have been applied. Readers may find some minor differences between terms used in the text and those which appear in the index. Suggestions to *sweetandmaxwell.taxonomy@thomson.com*

All entries are to paragraph number.

Index

Index